CHASING HUNGER

The 90 Day Bulimia Breakthrough Challenge

Kathy Welter Nichols

AuthorHouse™
1663 Liberty Drive
Bloomington, IN 47403
www.authorhouse.com
Phone: 1-800-839-8640

Published by AuthorHouse   01/26/2015

ISBN: 978-1-4969-1728-7 (sc)
ISBN: 978-1-4969-1727-0 (e)

Library of Congress Control Number: 2014910070

CONTENTS

Kathy Welter Nichols recommends:

The information given here is designed to help you make informed decisions about your body and health. The suggestions for specific foods, nutritional supplements, and exercise in the program are not intended to replace appropriate or necessary medical care. Before starting any new program always see your physician. If you have specific medical symptoms consult your physician immediately. If any recommendations given in this program contradict your physicians' advice, be sure to consult him or her before proceeding.

"Gold medals aren't really made of gold. They're made of sweat, determination, And a hard-to-find alloy called guts." ~ Unknown

DEDICATION

This book is dedicated to my wonderful
clients; each who have struggled
to make sense of their world and free themselves
from this debilitating addiction.
Thank you for sharing your journey
with me and helping me
blaze this new trail for others to follow.

Also to my daughters and grandchildren that they
might choose to be free of addictive behaviors and
know themselves as eternal beings of light.

With love and thanks to my husband Harry
Nichols for his love, patience and belief in me.

INTRODUCTION

In North America today one in three people knows someone with an eating disorder. Its epidemic, it's hidden, it's secretive. Recently eating disorders topped the highest mortality rate of any of the psychological disorders. Yes, higher than drug users, higher than depression, higher than alcoholism, in fact 20% higher in mortality rates than all other areas of psychological disorders.

In writing this book I've created nine separate challenges with tips, tools and exercises to help you. They are based on my work with these disorders over the past twelve years. Recovery is not easy, but you can achieve it. Whether you are in a program or endeavoring to stop on your own it's time to stop Chasing Hunger and start following a new path of health and wellness.

You may not believe that any treatment can restore you to sanity around food or get rid of the cravings for sugar, carbohydrates and binging. You may not even want to believe it's possible. You might find my challenge that you can help yourself recover from this debilitating world you currently live in, a wild claim. I appreciate you might be a little skeptical of another program.

Twelve years ago I saw my first client with bulimia. Her go to food was cookies. We easily removed cookies from her diet using NLP. It seemed that should have been the end of it, however, it just removed the target food. Now we had to address the underlying issues with self-esteem, anxiety, fear, panic and how she viewed herself. We had just started to touch the issues with speaking her truth, asking for what she wanted, believing she was safe in the world, OK to be herself, and trusting herself. Gradually seeing clients one on one evolved to a three day intensive using NLP (Neuro Linguistic Programming) and hypnosis. The good news was a majority of my clients secured the changes and walked away from bulimia just using the three day intensive. Since then I've added a 90 day weekly follow up with clients too.

Some clients were on various medical prescriptions and the program worked equally well for them too. The best results with the most powerful recovery times were achieved when the recommendations and suggestions for various supplements and an eating plan based on the diabetic, or glycemic index eating plan, were followed. The supplements assist in re-balancing the system and make good sense when endeavoring to assist your body through the early stages of recovery. This of course is all based on the understanding you are ready to walk away from bulimia for the last time and it's surprisingly easier than you think.

NLP and hypnosis are still profoundly effective for treating root causes of anxiety and panic attacks, post-traumatic stress, depression, obsessive compulsive disorders, weight loss and a whole host of other issues too, all of which are part of the world of someone with an eating disorder. Eventually shifting the sessions over three days to an "intensive" increased results dramatically as we overwhelmed bulimia and it had no place to resurface in the client's life. The three days allowed us to target the issues, problems, worries; fears, anxieties, and obsessive panic that they had believed were causing bulimia. Bulimia wasn't needed if they followed the program. In fact bulimia nicely retreats if you stop the restrictive diet.

This can seem like a miracle as clients shift this old behavior. And yet what is a Miracle? Miracles are like magic in action, wherever there is a break in what is believed facilitating the leap to what is possible.

Other clients shared they had bulimia and had gotten over it themselves. One of the great tools of NLP is in modeling behavior, replicating the sequences to attain similar outcomes. Asking others how they did it helped me refine the process until I had all the pieces to help my clients achieve similar results. If they followed the steps, the results were attainable.

It started with recognizing how they thought about their past behaviors. It was vastly different from the clients with this disorder:

"I realized one day, this was just a waste of time. My life was totally centered on this behavior I was sick of being sick. I just didn't have time for bulimia anymore. It takes up your whole life, you know. I realized this was really a teenage disorder; it

wasn't "in" to still be doing bulimia every day, and be in my thirties. It certainly wasn't controlling my weight anymore. (This is common I've obese bulimic clients too, as there is a point when it stops working for weight loss) It just made no sense to me anymore. I had been eating regularly so that wasn't a problem for me anymore. I just continued out of habit. One day I was going to do it, and I just didn't and that was it. I decided enough was enough and I was done with this. Bulimia just made no sense at all; in fact I guess it never really did".

How do you feel about bulimia in your life right now? What would have to change for you to feel the way this woman felt about it? What would you have to say to yourself? How would you feel about yourself? What would your life look like without bulimia, right now?"

HOW TO USE THIS BOOK:
THE 90 DAY CHALLENGE:

I recommend you take your time, and use each Challenge as if you were seeing me and working with me in the three day intensive. Each Challenge offers its own set of tips, tools and exercises for you to work through. I suggest you do them in sequence, as they are designed to build on each other. While you might entertain rushing through this in a weekend, I encourage you to relax and integrate each Challenge. Master each one. Understand it fully and apply it to your personal recovery and wellness path. You might continue to use your eating disorder while you are reading this book, that's perfectly OK too, as you work through this process, the eating disorder will simply make less and less sense to you.

You can use this book over and over again, each time you will achieve more awareness to help yourself. And you can also choose to read the whole thing through first and then come back to the beginning and start each challenge – one at a time applying the tools and integrating the process for you.

I've created MP3s and a Card Deck to help you, on the web site. They are easy to access and simple to use.

www.waysofthewisewoman.com and
www.chasinghunger.com

NOTES AS I BEGIN THIS WORK

Bulimia is something you want to stop, it's an addictive habit, and it's undermining your health and happiness and destroying your sense of confidence and success; you know that stopping this destructive addictive behavior will improve the quality of your life in so many ways.

Take a moment here and write down your current state. What do you believe about your current situation? What do you want right now? What stops you from getting that? How will you know you have achieved what you want? Is there anyone in your life right now that does not support your recovery?

_____

_____

_____

_____

_____

_____

Making a new start:

You may not believe this right now, however, as you awake in the morning, before you get out of bed, stretch in your bed with your eyes closed, and say these words to yourself....

"I accept myself just as I am"

This might be really challenging, you may have done some things that you regret doing, you may feel guilty and like this statement is not true. That's OK; I want you to start using this internal mantra now, every day. Whenever you get into a challenging moment, just stop and hear your own voice saying these words:

"I accept myself just as I am"

CHALLENGE 1

STARTING OVER, BACK
TO THE BASICS

This is a new beginning an initiation and a new start; you are the spark that ignites the mighty flame. A new sense of purpose is there within you - striking out alone drives your individuality and initiative, it always has. There are new beginnings possible as you once again pioneer independently of others. Sensing that incredible determination, and self-reliance as an energy force of great originality. It's time to stop listening to others about fast weight loss and begin to treat your body intuitively with respect and appreciation. Speed diets, fast weight loss schemes we know they don't work and now we know these old patterns are damaging to the core systems of the body, mind and spirit.

Eating is more than just food; it's the right food, at the right time and in right portion sizes

"Eating to live and not living to eat": The extensive and intense restricting of food is known to cause most of the symptoms of bulimia. Eating "normally" has been so confused by the world of "diets" we have to start here. The plan is for 90 days, eating the way the 90 day challenge suggests and

1

allowing food to become *just fuel*. **This challenge is to
eat 3 small meals a day, protein rich and 3 protein rich
snacks in between** *while stopping the consumption of junk
food: processed sugars and processed carbohydrates.*

Let's get started:

There are some fundamental problems with using bulimia
as a weight loss program and here are some of them:

- You cannot control other aspects of the brain/body
  response to counteract for the bulimic behavior.
- Over production of steroids create the puffy round
  moon-face so after binging and purging the face
  appears "fat".
- Obesity and diabetes are a reality; eventually
  bulimia stops controlling weight as systems break
  down
- Amenorrhea; losing your monthly cycle can lead
  to infertility as well as osteopenia and osteoporosis
  as your bone density is slowly leeched without the
  proper regular menses and hormones supplying it.
- The stomach is swollen and soft from binging,
  purging and heavy restricting. You have a continual
  bulge of bloating due to the stress hormone cortisol
  and from consuming high volumes of sugar and
  junk food and it will not go away.
- Skin is sallow and dark circles appear under the
  eyes, as a result of liver and kidney stress.

- Your heart is suffering, potassium levels fall to deathly levels, and your physical symptoms are dangerous.
- Hair can fall out, become dull and lifeless; teeth and throat are damaged from acid reflux.
- Low energy, short term memory loss and no energy are the daily normal.
- No one trusts you; your word doesn't mean much, most of your friends are people with the same lack of commitment to other people's time. You find you are often dumped, forgotten or just left out. You use bulimia and isolation instead.
- Negative mood swings are common you just don't have any resources to manage the simplest interactions and these moods often get taken out on the people who love you the most.
- Bulimia uses all your available cash and working the simplest job is hard as you have no energy and it seems you are always making excuses and apologizing for yourself to others
- You have adopted the attitude of what goes in must come out, so you don't use supplements or take very good care of your body in other ways either.
- Brain chemistry alters further as survival mode kicks in, obsessions about food, thinking about food, planning for binges, all drive the anxiety, tension and fear, which centers on the primary focus of planning "my next fix".
- Sugar gives you the high and also the depleted extreme lows, depression is common, feelings of low self-worth, obsessions around thinness and the

fear of weight gain "did I eat too much, did I get it all out? What is normal?"

- The over use of laxatives cause major issues with the colon and bowel.
- Moral components fall away to the power of the addiction; lying, stealing and waste which you never would have considered before become a part of everyday life.
- Aspects of the personality "split off" endeavoring to survive and the behavior itself becomes mindless and soul pillaging.
- Emotional issues are dealt with through bulimia, so you never resolve or master experience, you use bulimia instead. Anger sits uncomfortably just below the surface, vaguely masked by bland expressions.
- As bulimia depletes essential nutrients and amino acids it affects mood swings increasing isolation, fear, self-judging and robbing you of the ability to control impulses. GABA an essential amino acid drives impulses that are out of control; yeast overgrowth occurs from the sugars, carbohydrates and lack of protein which drive the system into frenzy. *I must have my daily fix.*
- You don't know how to stop. You try, but you never do it. As behavior escalates the damages increase; panic attacks, unnecessary fears, emotional outbursts as the brain craves its daily fix.
- Bulimia seemed like a good idea for weight loss; however, no matter what movies you watched, books

you read or suggestions from others; CHASING HUNGER is simply no way to lose weight.

How do we stop this addictive behavior?

This is it: **Stop using bulimia for 90 days,** and commit to use these challenges to overcome and correct these unresourceful behaviors, then continue and stop *Chasing Hunger* for the rest of your life. The first challenge is to eat again. This challenge is to eat three small protein rich meals a day, along with protein rich snacks and then *keeping it. While refraining from processed sugars and processed carbohydrates.*

"Eating to live and not living to eat": The new plan. One that works 100% of the time, you won't really have to think about it much at all, soon you will notice you are not obsessing about food either, in fact you won't even be thinking about it.

OBJECTIONS:

"My bowels don't work properly and that's always been a problem. I feel bloated. My clothes are too tight. Eliminating doesn't seem to happen often enough or in enough volume. I've used so many laxatives. I've really damaged my bowel and I need help or otherwise I have pain, bloating and get really nervous about weight gain. I already have a way I choose to eat, and it works for me. I have my good days, I know what they are and how to do this, and I don't want to start another restrictive program. I'm afraid if I eat this much, I'm going to gain weight."

Bulimia starts with a strategy of restricting food over long periods of time during the hormonal teen years when the brain is already undergoing massive changes affecting personality, emotional development and the physical body. As teenagers we think everyone around us has it all together, they seem to have this figured out. We feel like we don't fit in, and our clothes seem the reflection of that feeling, they don't fit us from one year to the next. If we opt for an addiction at this age, we entrain belief that can last a lifetime, and it's based on experiences during times when our brain was undergoing massive changes and we felt powerless to affect our immediate experience.

It starts innocently enough with a diet to lose weight. "This is a way I can control, my body's weight gains, and it seems to get everyone's approval too". We have all done it and that's testimony to the billion dollar diet industry we have today. Any self-help section in any book store will produce the latest fad diets and ways to lose a quick 10 or 20 pounds. When we *feel* we don't fit in, are awkward, make mistakes, parents and siblings are no support; we think *what if I lost 50 pounds? In fact how thin can I get?*

With no clear exit strategy in place, excessive restricting of calories goes on and on and your brain and body are now triggered into "starvation mode". Remember food is fuel; it fuels our body's energy. Calories are units of energy. And you are still growing. With no clear exit strategy from a diet gone horribly wrong, the continued restricting catapults the body into starvation and once you lose control of restricting, you are into full on panic and binge eating.

No matter what movies you watched, books you read or suggestions from others; CHASING HUNGER is simply no way to lose weight.

What would the life you want to live, be like?

If you could imagine the life you want right now, what would be in it? First you would have to know what you want. Let yourself do this right now and imagine it in full color, with the sounds you might hear, and the tones that would make you feel amazing inside. Stretch your imagination and if you hit that inner roadblock "well I can't because of...", just stop yourself and pretend - dream your dream life, right here:

What would having what you want be like?
What would you see?
What would you hear?
What would it feel like inside?
What changes would have to happen in your life?
What about your relationships?
Who would be in your social life?
How would finances improve?
What changes in your health?
Would you change where you live?
What would change at work or school?
What do you really want your life to be like?

Imagine having everything you want right now…
Write it down just the way you want it. The more detail
the better.

Where do we start? Right here:

Eat six times during the day, 3 small protein rich meals and
three small protein rich snacks between the meal times so
you are essentially eating every 2-3 hours.

Start within thirty minutes after you get up in the morning,
eat your first meal of the day, and your body will set your
metabolic rate for the day. When you skip breakfast, saving
yourself for a binge at night, you also miss this major calorie
burning signal your body naturally sets as your metabolic
rate for the day. This tells the body *here's the rate to efficiently
burn my caloric intake today.* If you starve yourself first thing
in the morning you waste this great auto-calorie burner.
Eat within 30 minutes of rising to balance your insulin and
blood sugar, and set your metabolic rate for the day.

When we skip breakfast, insulin levels spike and then drop
leaving you feeling weak, light headed, and unable to think
clearly.

Begin to notice when your brain sends images of food; this
is when the body is experiencing hunger. It should be about
every two to three hours. When your brain starts sending
you images of food, it's telling you the resources inside
are getting low. This is generally the moment you used to
check with your tummy and decide – "no, I'll wait a while

and plan what I'll be eating later tonight". This is the start of the inner war between you and your body, because you are not listening to the real cues. The more you stay on routine with 3 small protein rich meals a day and 3 protein snacks between meals, the more your body will balance and stabilize. If you feed your body protein every 2-3 hours you will experience a huge difference. Even "healthy" big salads with just veggies lack protein you are going to feel very hungry in about 20 minutes. Add some chicken, fish, eggs, beans, quinoa or meat and you will see a big difference. You won't be thinking about food at all. Your body needs the protein.

Test this; eat your protein first, wait a few moments after eating, and check... am I thinking about food now? "No, I'm not thinking about food, *hey this works.*"

Now: Add in supplements and vitamins, and a walk each night after dinner, even just 20 minutes and get some good movement going. This is helpful for insulin uptake and will remove those habit patterns of binging later in the evening.

A Candida supplement will assist with cravings for wheat and sugar resulting from an over production of yeast in your system. Try to avoid any cleanses right now, because these can be very hard on your recovering system. It's better to bring in support through supplements. Review the ingredients of your foods and discard anything with fructose, sucrose, dextrose and corn syrup these are the products that are more addictive that street heroin.

The body only registers a small signal with fried foods, chips, junk food, sugars etc., Restricting fuel can trigger starvation later in non-stop binging behaviors. Remember survival is below your conscious awareness and your brain will do everything it can to keep you alive, even accepting these junk foods and sugars as fuel to keep going. A small portion of protein every few hours will give you greater control around portion sizes and food choices. We now know that restricting alone will not effectively lose weight.

Perhaps if we designated these "foods" as not being "real food" it would help us discern what food really is. Real food is our fuel. Food is really just meant to be fuel. It's not a reward system or a way to self-harm, it's just fuel. Food is just fuel.

Discard the junk sugars

When scientists figured out how to split the sugar molecule, they valued the nucleus while discarding the carbons of the sugar molecule as 'junk'. Soon industry discovered the junk sugars are the delivery system within the sugar molecule and they pack a big punch. Realizing "junk" sugars are excellent preservatives and about 100 times sweeter than the whole glucose molecule it started to appear in everything.

Note: your brain needs the glucose: **the whole sugar molecule** and you get this in some vegetables and all fruits, it's whole and complete. Eat fruit in moderation along with protein to balance blood sugars and support your brain in recovery. Adding fruit to your diet, you won't miss the sweet or feel like you can't have a sweet. Our gustatory sensory system reads salt, savory, sweet, sour and translates that for the brain. The brain responds with positive feedback loops, and so if you endeavor to eliminate one of these completely (all sugar is banded) the body will crave it. Instead, chose your sweets from fruit and you won't get caught in that negative feedback generating a craving for sugar.

These junk sugars are labeled: fructose, sucrose, dextrose and corn syrup. Stop buying them. And the only way you will know is to read the ingredients label on the side of the package.

Chemicals to leave on the shelf: mono-sodium glutamate (MSG), hydrolyzed soy protein, auto-lyzed yeast extract, fructose, dextrose, sucrose and corn syrup or any chemical that you need a computer to find out what it is. If you don't know what it is, how can your body deal with breaking it down and using it for fuel?

Foods to avoid where possible:

Margarines: Fats from oils are trans-fats and create a hormonal imbalance, depleting the Adepenectin in the body. **This is the hormone that regulates your metabolism.** Protein rich pumpkin seeds regulate and restore this hormone.

Sugar: It's in everything, read your labels. Eliminate fructose, sucrose and dextrose & corn syrup. Junk sugar, is stored in the brain, creating intense sugar cravings, foggy thinking and memory loss; sugar is a legal and lethal drug.

Limit whole wheat, breads and pastas: Genetically Modified foods in North America cause all kinds of digestive issues for many. New research is indicating the long term accumulative effects of these foods are showing up in diseases of the gut.

How to reduce Cortisol: *Breathe!!* Yes, breathing deeply, 4 – 5 times in a stressful moment, will redirect the body into the relaxation response, which helps reverse cortisol – the stress hormone. Add a few deep breaths when you feel stressed or tired. Adding daily meditation will also increase the relaxation response. (More to follow on adding this value packed practice to your life)

Reduce soy intake, the chemicals used to create soy products sadly outweigh any benefit our body receives from the soy. It's high in estrogen producing chemicals, which slows metabolism while increasing weight gain and changing our female hormones. Until they change the process, leave this one on the shelf.

Orange Juice and fruit juices: A regular sized freshly squeezed orange juice has the juice of about 5 oranges in it- eat one whole fruit instead and benefit from the fiber too.

EXERCISE FOR THIS CHALLENGE:

1: Eat three small meals during the day, proteins first and three protein rich snacks in between
2: Eat between 7 am and 7pm and eat slowly with intention
3: Notice when the body is experiencing hunger -listen to your body – why does it want wheat or sugar? When was the last time you gave it food?
4: Add in the recommended supplements and vitamins – every day
5: Add in a walk each night after dinner, for optimum insulin uptake

Suggested times of the day to eat

A good rule of thumb is 80% of your daily intake is between 7 am and 7 pm. This will alleviate the excessive snacking and food consumption that often goes on in the evenings and it ensures your body has enough energy to take care of all its tasks for the day.

Eat breakfast 30 minutes after you rise (sets the metabolism for the day – your personal auto fat buster)
Eat a snack 2-3 hours later
Eat lunch at 12-1pm
Eat a snack 2-3 hours later and eat dinner 2-3 hours later with a small snack before bed

Keep larger meals to the middle of the day; include an evening walk to assist with insulin uptake and balance blood sugar levels before bed. (This will reduce night "snacking" helping you maintain your freedom from nightly binging and purging and increase a deep sleep).

Suggested Portion Sizes

This can be everyone's issue really, *how much*? How much is too much? When have I had too much? When do I stop? What if I'm still hungry? How much is the right amount for me?

It's right there in the palms of your hands. And it's your palms, your hands, not your moms, dads, or the waiter or the chef in the kitchen that never even sees you. *It's your hands.*

The size and thickness of the palm of one hand is the size for your protein. That's the amount of steak, chicken, meat, fish or eggs, just that much: One palm, on one hand, size and thickness.

The size of one hand cupped is for cooked rice, potatoes, pasta, or any cooked food.

Two hands cupped for the raw salad, veggies etc.

You might think that is a very small amount of food, but wait, you are eating *six times a day*. Is that too much food you might think: three meals, three snacks? No its just the right amount. What if you eat a bit more at one meal than another, that's OK we'll balance that out with the 80/20 rule…

The benefit here is: food in every 2-3 hours, eaten slowly for just 20 minutes and you may not finish it all. Protein and nutrient rich, *food becomes fuel.*

Suggestions for changing how you eat

Use a small fork and a small plate or bowl. Follow the recommended portion sizes, right there in the palms of your hands. *Yes. Let food go to waste*, rather than to your waist it's *perfectly OK. (an optimum use of the word "perfect")*

In this way your body will take itself to its right weight and you won't even have to monitor or measure anything *ever again.* During this re-feeding time use acidophilus or probiotics, taken as recommended about 15 minutes before each meal. It will help re-balance the gut and you will find the bloating and the digestive process easing. This will take time; give yourself the full 90 days to re-balance this.

Eat slowly; put your fork down between bites. Take your time, slow the process, and make this a new habit. Eating slowly, taking the longest amount of time, to finish the smallest amount of food. Eat for 20 minutes, and when 20 minutes is complete, stop eating. Your comfort zone should feel neither hungry, nor over full, truly comfortable. Check in with your tummy. Breathe and relax the tummy muscles. You are done eating for this "meal" and will be eating again in 2-3 hours. Eventually the mind body connections will indicate the signal, "I'm getting low on food - sending food images to the mind"

And this will correlate to approximately the time of every 2-3 hours.

Supplements to help you through these 90 days:

Take all as recommended- remember more is not better, it's often just more

Add a **Candida supplement** to assist with sugar cravings and re-balance any Candida overgrowth

Add in **L-Glutamine & GABA** daily (eat red meat – grass fed –if it's right for you)

Add in **DHA** supplement, fish oils for brain development & support

Add in **Vitamins B & C 1000** each day (ESTER-C is best – easy to absorb)

Add in **Vitamin D,** to support immune system

Magnesium before bed relieves constipation and Dandelion for deep restful sleep

Bach Flower Remedies: *Walnut* for transitions, and *Gorse* to relieve a feeling of hopelessness

Add in **Coconut Water** daily to re-balance low potassium levels

Avoid any cleanses right now, while your bowel and gut are in recovery mode

Food with fructose, sucrose, dextrose and corn syrup – discard them all. Just throw them away. Wherever these are listed, just remove it from your house. These are the products that are more addictive than heroin and will fuel your sugar addiction.

Eat before you shop and shop from a list

Shopping lists: This is one of the top recommendations from those that have recovered: Shop with a shopping list as it gives you control over what you are spending on food. Use a list. Keep your list handy in your kitchen and when you are going shopping for food, take the list. Do not buy any food items not on the list. If you see something you need, just turn the list over and write it on the back, it's the start of your new shopping list (you can also use your cell phone for your list) In this way you never buy something that is an "impulse" instead you are shopping from the list – you have control. This eliminates anxiety around shopping, giving you complete control and saves your budget too.

Eat before you go food shopping, you won't be hungry and your blood sugar will remain constant giving you enough energy and focus to stay on task. You won't come home with foods that won't help you maintain your 90 day challenge. We're eating real food here, the kind that someone would eat to help their body be healthy, strong and energized. Consider it critical to "eat before you go shopping" so you are not starving in the grocery store and buying things you don't want. This is why it's a *best plan* to have a shopping list and *eat before you go shopping.*

Organizing your fridge: clean and wash your fridge thoroughly. As you do this task take a moment and read the labels checking ingredients and the expiry date on the products. Discard any foods that fall into the categories with junk sugar or are past the sell-by-date.

Your body is not a garbage can, time to stop treating yourself like one. Your body is the one thing you have that is totally yours for this lifetime. Give it the best food and endeavor to find out what those are. Care enough to want the best for your body; this is the key to your 90 day challenge. So clear these foods out of your fridge and don't buy them anymore.

Taking control of your kitchen: Why read labels? The government has set out laws that the food industry must label all foods, so we know what's in them, and if they don't, they face some big fines. It's important. Generally the middle aisles of the grocery store are where all the food additives are. These are the foods that must have labels so read them.

It's helpful for you to know what these things mean, in fact these substances affect how crazy you get around food, and some of the things in the foods you have been eating are in part, responsible for your complete lack of control around food. Food sensitivities can make us behave quite differently to who we really are. It's like there's a monster side that comes out, and begins to consume everything in front of us. If you know what they are, then you can choose other foods and this will help you remain in control of your recovery. It means you have to take time in the grocery store and read the labels on the foods you are purchasing.

Suggestion: obtain glass containers for storage in your fridge

You can see your beautiful foods easily. Plastic can be easily absorbed into the food so, choose glass instead. The cheaper the plastic the more chances of some really dangerous chemicals getting into your foods. Open your fridge door and when you stand in front of it, look at the shelf that is at eye level. This is the shelf that can hold all the "ready to eat" foods that you have purchased, washed, cleaned and placed into the glass containers. They just beam at you when you open the door. Vegetables, fruits, hummus, hard boiled eggs, salad and greens are all inviting when prepared at the time of purchase, and stored in glass.

The lower shelves: Store Meat, fish, and other foods that need preparation on these shelves. It's OK to shop daily for food rather than doing big purchases in large quantities. In fact it's a wonderful way to support your recovery shopping daily for healthy foods.

Organizing your pantry: Sort through these foods as well, look through the ingredients and check all the nutrients, these packaged foods are often high in the substances that cause you to go out of control with your eating. Discard the junk sugar, and if you feel bad about throwing food away, give it away. Often tinned foods are the worst for sugars, preservatives and high sodium. Have a look and just put them in a bag to give away or discard. Dry cereals all have sweeteners; check what kind of sugars are in the foods you are eating. These will trigger a lot of negative reactions for you and you can easily find ones that don't – reading the label helps you make better choices.

How red meat counteracts a lot of these problems (and only if it is compatible for you)

Before you say "just another fix, I struggled to give up red meat" take look at this:

We deplete the brain eating sugars, starving it of the proteins and nutrients needed which are the building blocks of the cells. Restricting, vegan and vegetarian diets can also begin to drive binge behavior. When clients follow the diabetic eating plan, or something like the Paleo diet, eating more protein, it immediately restores balance, allows for greater control and releases the drive for sugars and carbohydrate fixes. This can seem a big compromise if you have moved away from animal based protein, however, if you have then endeavor to ensure you are eating proteins from vegetable sources at each meal and snack. It will be a little more challenging, however, there is lots of help in these areas today with smoothies.

Recently a client shared she had a day of rushing with her food times - missing a few meals, and by 6pm that evening she felt like binging and purging. She'd been free of the thoughts and triggers for over three weeks, and suddenly, she was panicking. When we reviewed what she had eaten that day it was only carbohydrates, sugars and zero protein, and not very much volume either. I recommended she "double up on proteins" right then. So she made some scrambled eggs and a steak, and that put her right back in control. Sometimes we need these experiences because it clearly indicates what is actually triggering behaviors. We have not been treating food as fuel. The following day, she was right back on her eating plan and it completely finished with this for her going forward. She knew exactly what to do to keep on her wellness plan.

Choose grass fed beef, free range chicken and eggs then bless and be grateful

L-Glutamine, GABA, Serotonin, and Dopamine are the areas that become deficient

When we reduce the sugar & carbohydrates some other things begin to happen for a short while:

We can experience an increase in the drive for other addictive components, the pleasure centers of the brain want their fix, so take your time, have patience with all of this, especially with how you think things should be going, relax and trust the process, here its time to add in fruit and vegetables as it will off-set that craving for sweet.

Resources for interrupting binge eating, food cravings and compulsive eating:

The anxious state creates a predisposition for cravings and
      sugar fixes
What is going on physically? What do I want to calm myself
      with?
Examining the Bio-Chemistry of what stimulates the desire
Fear of Food: "What if I?" thinking, obsessions and
      restricting all drive this intensity
Brain Chemistry is affected: *we have to have something*
When we stop eating the sugary foods, there can be slight
      levels of depression associated with this, so you may feel
      a little low, low energy, tired; however, this is a good sign
      your body is clearing these toxins from your brain. Keep
      going you are in recovery.

Symptoms associated with low production of Dopamine, GABA & Serotonin

Low energy, tired, blood sugar erratic, insulin imbalance,
carbohydrate cravings, diabetes, low blood sugar, hypo
glycemic, obesity, feel worthless, feeling depressed a drive
for pleasure seeking and attention seeking behaviors: crave
sugar; isolate socially, lack of follow through, low tolerance
for stress, procrastinate, confused thinking, loss of memory,
feel depressed, something is wrong with me, I don't fit in
like everyone else.

Your body is working hard to re-balance and reaches for sugar trying to bring itself back into homeostasis, or balance with consuming "instant energy" from sugar.

GABA: Is a major inhibitor in the brain, keeps bio chemicals in check

When this is depleted, we can get obsessed with foods, diet and just about everything
Sleep/anxiety/nervous, craving carbohydrates and obsessive anxious behaviors
Serotonin: (is a natural inhibitor) and helps curb cravings for:
Alcohol, drugs, salt, lashing out, impulsive behaviors, anger even rage

How do we deplete neuro transmitters?

Mental stress, multi-tasking, keeping busy, doing too many things, on the phone, skipping meals, not sleeping, over exercise, artificial sugars; *I hate boredom I must keep busy.*

Testing the neurotransmitter levels:

Essential fatty acids are so important, Omega 3 & 6 are often depleted through years of restricting and bulimic behavior. Add in the Omega supplements here to help the brain begin recovery.

The pattern of self-pleasuring and rewarding after intense restricting are similar to any drug use like heroin, alcohol or cocaine; it releases the *feel good* chemical release, and hits the reward centers of the brain. "I've got my fix". Junk sugar will increase these cravings, increase withdrawal, and cross sensitization to other addictive chemicals; so the more sugar we eat, the more we crave substances that reward these same centers. Morphine, cocaine, alcohol, nicotine and junk sugar all affect the same centers of the brain.

This starts to go way out of balance, driven by restricting and then rewarding with binging so the brain becomes a slave to the entrained patterns of bulimia.

Protein has amino acids; arginine stimulates growth, decreases fat

Use cinnamon, chromium, protein snacks, instead of artificial sweeteners

Wheat & Dairy - often this can be an allergy as gluten has an opiate response as well

Portion size; use your hands as your measuring tool eat slowly, with focus and appreciation

Three small meals a day with three small snacks in between, protein rich and you will begin to re balance your body. The benefits of following the Glycemic Index Eating plan, or the basic Diabetic Eating Plan, (3 small meals and 3 small snacks) as your body will go to its right weight. You can permanently leave behind the belief you need to be doing something to your body to make that happen. Your body is a smart system; it knows how to do this for you.

Compulsions around food: The compulsion blow out

What food causes you the most problem? Pick one that you cannot refuse, one that if you think of it, you are going to have to go get it. One of your serious compulsion foods, maybe ice cream or pizza.

How intense is that compulsion?

From 0-10, how strong is that feeling in you when you think of that food?

Give it a number _____?

Bring that image to mind now:

- Notice how big it is, is it moving? Is it a still image, or is it moving like in a movie? Does it have a smell attached to it? Can you taste it? Does it make your mouth water?
- How close is the image? Could you reach out and touch it?
- Is it in full color? Is it in black and white?
- If you bring the image up close, and make it very large does it make it more compelling? What number is it right now from 0-10 _____?

Now, quickly ***take all of the color out of the image.***

> It could take a moment, watch as the color drains away from the image, look back at the image and notice the image is now black and white.
>
> Can you make it a ***Still image*** and put a border around the image – just a boring picture. Go ahead and make the edges all fuzzy and out of focus, gray and dull.
>
> Now ***shrink*** the image down to a small dot. Imagine "flicking it away" with your thumb and finger. Push it away from you.
>
> Take a deep breath and just check in with your feelings...

What's the number now? _____? If this number is not zero repeat until it is.

- To completely remove this compulsion, so this food will never again be of any interest to you,
- Recall the last time you vomited it up? There it is in full colour in the toilette bowl.
- Imagine how that food looks right now, and how it smells and what it felt like in your mouth as you were vomiting it into the toilette.
- Now think of that food again ... do you feel more than slightly repulsed by this food?
- Notice how it smelled when you vomited it, and how it looked too, before you flushed it
- While this is not very pleasant, this will remove foods you used to binge on to induce vomiting

- Just keep repeating this mental imagery until this food holds no interest for you and in fact is repulsive to you
- Test it by going into a store and seeing foods you used to binge on, as black and white, strangely uncompelling, of no interest to you, in fact repulsive to you.

Use this quick visual collapse to neutralize a negative state:

Open both palms upright in front of you; imagine several powerful positive experiences you have had. Things you have done, achieved accomplished and remember how great you felt. Make the images bright, full colour and see yourself right in there. Hear what others were saying and the tone as you get those great feelings rolling through your body, feel the little tingles? Breathe into them and expand the feeling so it's moving all through you. Imagine stacking all that wonderful "feeling" and experience right there in the palm of your dominate hand. Feel what you were feeling and connect to that personal power that is you. Things where you felt just amazing about something you had done something that you were really proud of. Feel it now and breathe into that feeling, expanding that feeling so its moving through your body, and beginning to spiral up and down, feeling better and better as you move this energy through you.

Now imagine the negative feeling of perhaps fear or doubt, or even boredom, and put it there in your other hand and move this hand under the dominate hand holding all the wonderful energy from that amazing moment. Imagine pouring the entire contents of positive experiences from the dominate hand down, flowing over into the old negative experience in the other hand. Watch it just blow out the negative feelings. As the positive energy flows from one hand into the negative in the other, imagine all that feeling being completely overwhelmed and blown out by the positive states. When it's all gone, take a deep breath in and just reconnect the powerful flow spiraling all those wonderful feelings through your body again.

Take a moment now and bring your thumb and finger together on your dominant hand and press them together as you revisit this wonderful inner flow of incredible personal energy. Imaging yourself in your favorite colors and feel it moving through you just as it did in that moment. Amplify this spiraling feeling by taking a deep breath in, and now squeeze the thumb and finger together, anchoring this new positive resource state.

We all get anchored to certain events, certain places and certain moments in the day. Celebrations, banquets, in our own kitchen, and even at work in low energy times like 2 pm in the afternoon. To change this kind of "anchored" experience, you have to have something more compelling going on in the moment and not associated to foods.

At Work: Be sure you have eaten a snack mid-afternoon and have interesting projects to work on later in the day. You will find 5 pm is there before you know it. For all of us, this 'low energy time' of the day can be challenging. It's when the blood sugar levels in the body drop and fuel for your body and mind are needed. Changing this pattern is easier than you think, just like the person that always smokes in the same chair at home, move the chair and change the space around, have a different activity to do at that time of day, and this challenge is handled for you. Interrupt patterns that are not serving you by simply doing something else. That afternoon snack will help you regain control of the low blood sugar levels quickly and have more control over habituated rituals.

Routines that do not serve you create ritual and rule-bounded patterns of behavior. Simply change them, interrupt them, and make them harder to perform. By doing this you will begin the process of retraining your rule bounded rituals.

Supplements: For the next 90 days, add these into your daily diet: (please take all supplements as directed - taking more of anything is not better it's just more and often can cause other issues).

L-Glutamine, and GABA – these have been depleted through the binge/purge cycles and the food choices, both are available as supplements. Candida overgrowth intensifies the "itch for sugars". You can add in: **Candida supplement,**

Vitamin B-100 Complex, Vitamin C, Evening Primrose, and Vitamin E.

Bach flower remedy – Take 2 drops daily of each: Walnut for transition and Gorse for feelings of hopelessness. These really help.

CHALLENGE 2:

GOOD AND BAD, ENDING RULE BOUNDED THINKING

Duality and ridged rules require balance. Either or, good or bad create anxiety. Simultaneously two situations or options create the argument and you must decide. A choice is needed, which way will I choose? There is a love of beauty and a desire for peace often at the center of you, and often you feel upset trying to decide. Anxiety and panic arise as you try to do the right thing or make the perfect choice. Here we can choose another way and break the cycle. With applied wisdom gained through experience we can begin to lessen the black and white thinking, the rule bounded and the intensity of worry and anxiety around what bad thing might happen.

From Challenge One, you are now eating three small protein rich meals a day, plus three snacks between meals, between the hours of 7 am and 7 pm approximately every 2-3 hours, good flexibility while adding in supplements and using your personalized portion sizes there in the palms of your hands.

Small meals several times a day is optimum for fuel, enhancing the body's insulin uptake, digestion, and re-balancing the systems that have been ravaged by the "eating to purge" process. Portion sizes change everything; small meals every few hours re-balance the body.

Food is just fuel, it's just fuel; ending the battle of good or bad foods. *It's just fuel.*

OBJECTIONS:

I get really anxious around foods I think about food a lot, especially the foods I binge on, I'm out of control when I shop I go crazy around food and try to control what I eat, and then I lose it again What about my anxiety? What about my boredom? I try every day, and I fail

HOW BULIMIA STARTS: RESTRICT AND LIMIT FOOD INTAKE FOR THE PURPOSE OF LOSING WEIGHT — A DIET.

"On a bad day.... (A bulimia day) I awake feeling alarmed... Always feeling I need to clean up, not leave any trace, all must be perfect/in order/as was left but better with a blanket of peace and calm. Always anxiety and ruminating about leaving something... obviously not a deal breaker but it consumes my mind and energy. Needing to please, always do my best in performance and conversation, articulation, always the perfect order.

Bulimia can be mindless at best, becoming a growing entity in one's life; all-consuming thoughts are centered on the endless routines of its compulsion. It's simply become habituated in patterns of ritual and everything you do now, continues to support the habit. You might think in a reasonable moment, I'm worried about eating at all, because I can go crazy around food and I can't stop myself. However, that's the patterns of binging to purge and your brain knows just how to do this very well. What we need here is a way to break the duality and doing something different. Do one thing differently: The binging will stop when your body knows it's getting fed several times a day, and with real fuel.

"A non-bulimia day for me looks somewhat like this:

Upon rising: latte tea with unsweetened almond milk, carrot juice with greens or other vegetable juice with honey; mid-day - egg protein with almond or coconut milk. Afternoon - dried fruit (preferably unsweetened) and nuts; Dinner - miso soup with vegetable, veg salad with egg, dried or fresh turkey, Dulce seaweed, honey/olive oil/balsamic."

Good days or bad days there is not enough protein and too much sugar so even recovery days are sabotaged. Bulimia damages sleep (Serotonin levels), impulse control centers (GABA), and stimulates pleasure and reward centers in the body and brain. These entrained behaviors result in the mindless rituals that support remaining in the old "comfort zone" of bulimia. To break out of either or - good or bad rule bounded behaviors, do just one thing differently. When going to mom's for dinner, eat before you go. Eat *your* food, protein rich, and arrive relaxed and calm so you can focus on the people and the evening instead of the food.

Food is just fuel.

Clients have shared their doctors have suggested bulimia as a way to stop the anorexic restricting behavior; recommending they try bulimia, as some nutrient is absorbed through the digestive track before vomiting. Once the "restricting" is controlled through binging and purging, consuming vast quantities of food becomes the new normal. Real anxiety, panic and fear about gaining excessive weight reinforce the fear around stopping bulimia. Together with distorted thoughts and body systems struggling to function; reinforcing the reward system of the brain, this pattern is going to rob you of living any kind of 'normal' life. The idea of the diet is a long lost memory and planning for binging and purging 'what can I get' is the new normal day. Being good and resisting bad food choices are all just part of the never ending struggle with duality.

The way out: do one thing differently. Break the pattern by interrupting it and do something completely different.

Start with interrupting the old behaviors by maintaining focus on what you really want, with full imagery: fill in those images; make it bright, lively and compelling. Cancel comparison thinking as soon as it starts. Bring it to your awareness and recognize it "ah ha! There I go again, and I don't want that, I'm choosing to do something different this time!" Awareness: that old internal language pattern is going to get me the old beliefs and behaviors. I'm choosing to focus on my new life, the one I really want, the joy, the happiness, the life partner and friends. Seeing myself in the middle of the fun and pleasure and achieving what I really want.

Let's adjust those old compulsive thoughts: take all the color and light out of those images so it's shadowy, fading and not very appealing. I fact it's dark and gloomy, just how your life used to be. "I definitely don't want that anymore". Here your own voice supportive, kind and encouraging. "I can do this, of course I can, I really can do anything I chose to put my mind to".

Enough is enough; I'm done with that now.

Keeping commitments to yourself, following your personal wellness plan is so much brighter, healthy and self-loving and you feel great about yourself every day, and in every way, stronger, healthier as you move towards securing what you really want.

What to do when you experience anxiety eating with others

Emerging from an eating disorder can really leave us feeling vulnerable around just eating. The truth is as much as you want to just "eat normally", your normal has been so chaotic, its hard to know what that actually is. And it can feel like everyone is watching. "They are judging how much I'm eating, and if I will leave the table afterward and go purge. Everyone knows what I'm doing".

We can get right out of our body with this kind of anxiety and tension. It's also just as likely others are all focused on their own meals and really not that interested in you or what you are doing. In fact most people are focused on themselves almost 100% of the time. This is one of the best times to ensure you eat before you go out with others to eat. Yes, eat before the dinner party, eat protein, in small portion sizes. On arrival at the event, focus on connecting with three of your friends or family. Talk to them about something completely different. You will find there is zero anxiety, and food is really not that important to you. Others might declare how "hungry they are", and you can reflect and know you are perfectly satisfied and ready to eat just your "normal small portion size".

These are strategies that "work for you".

Making new decisions for myself

If food is fuel, and my body needs the fuel to optimize it's functions, and I'm in control of what I give or do not give to my body, then it falls to me and only me to take full responsibility for what goes in and when.

Sometimes we feel a lot of guilt or shame around eating, and the way we've used food in the past, or we've been really resistant to others telling us when to eat, and how much. That's OK, that was then; this is now. As you begin to eat three small meals and three small snacks, protein rich, approximately every three hours, your body is going to begin to relax around food. Anxiety will begin to diminish and you will become more emotionally balanced and be able to visit with others; instead of being anxious, in your head and wanting to isolate yourself away from everyone.

This is my body I do know what is right for me

Other people may remind you: *"We were so worried about you dear… are you sure you are eating the right amount and why so many times in the day? Is that right? Who told you this…?"* These kinds of comments can really trigger anxiety and tension, especially if it's with someone that is close to us; here it's perfectly OK to set a boundary.

"I know what I'm doing, and I know what is right for my body. This is working for me, and I'm content with following this. Please support me in my changes and recovery."

One client's mom and dad owned a fitness studio and had a very successful program helping people train and sculpt their bodies. Their students had won many competitions and this reflected on their business. The process they recommended was: three *solid big meals a day and nothing else*: they had their family follow their "rules" too. Of course the company paid all the bills and so everyone in the family that benefited from the company's financial gains was "obligated" to participate in this way. In the first meeting with mom and her daughter, it was evident the controls were very tight around food, feeding times and any changes to that process would meet with objection.

Mom began with her worries and anxiety around changing any of the feeding routines. *"This is the way we do it; we have so many clients that are so successful; I've maintained my weight for years doing exactly this. I don't want her eating six times a day, she will definitely get fat."*

When I suggested the glycemic eating plan is healthy and very successful for recovery, in fact it's the recommended eating plan for diabetics; we follow it for balancing blood sugar and insulin uptake. She hit me with her final blow: *"well, she'll gain weight, there is just no question, eating six times a day she will definitely gain weight."*

The daughter blanched and looked at me with anxious eyes, I knew it was her greatest fear and she simply would not, could not eat the portion sizes they put in front of her every day. Their food portions were never in accordance with listening to her body. The three large portion sized meals, eaten daily were much more than her small frame could comfortably manage; so she ate it all and threw it up. I advised her mother that the portion sizes should be smaller especially as were working on healing her irritable bowel as well, so smaller meals more often is the best way to go.

I would like to say, that a lot of people would never even think of commenting on what someone else is eating. Why would they? It's not their body. It's when we get into the belief that *someone else's way of eating might be better for us*, or what someone else is doing like a diet, might be the way to go. This is a recipe for trouble it's outside your own body. There's no point at looking at someone else's rules around food and making them your own. Even recommendations in diet books fall to this - how can one diet/portion size, cover every body, size, frame, density, age, culture and/or belief strategy? And why do we listen to these recommendations and try to make them ours? It's completely illogical.

Your portion sizes, right there in your hands.

Some families think offering guidance about food and food intake is helpful, it's not. This client was 24 years of age and living away from home at school. The long arm of the family business was still trying to enforce their rules.

A good use of the artful *pattern interruption:* When confronted with a situation where you are being pressured into talking about something you'd rather not. Interrupt the conversation by introducing another subject. Maybe ask about their new scarf, hair style or job. Or better yet, ask them about something you know they love to talk about.

Just ask them a question and it interrupts the pattern and re-directs the conversation. Parents often forget when we're 28 or 30 years old, we will remember our umbrella and we won't lose our house keys. If we've been indulging in an eating disorder for years, it's a constant irritant to the family, especially your parents because they view everything you do as a failure *in them and they often try to show support through over managing your recovery. It's not helpful.*

This is a way of creating new boundaries and they will keep directing and commenting until you say stop, and still they may not. It's a habit for them too. Some mothers start worrying when you are born and it's their pattern, *"if I don't worry, I worry something bad will happen to her".* Letting go gently sometimes just isn't possible and you need to be strong and support these new boundaries and reinforce them. "No this is my work now and I'm doing it". Remember we learn these anxious patterns from someone, and if your mother soothed her anxiety by trying to control you, then you will need to know how to effectively interrupt her patterns.

One mother asked me not to interrupt her daughter's habit for drinking wine. I had permission to deal with all other foods and aspects of bulimia, but not the wine, "that's the one thing we really enjoy together". Mom had a problem with wine. The daughter was diabetic and while she was told by her doctor, one glass of wine once in a while was not a problem; one glass... the habitual pattern between mother and daughter was to drink a bottle or two a night. When the daughter was on her own, she still consumed a bottle of wine a night, and then raged in anger at her mother and everyone else for her health problems and having bulimia.

Suggestion: Eat before going out with friends or family

Adopting new behaviors is like taking a new lease on life. Start with *food as fuel*. Just sitting down at the table to eat with friends facing a pile of food can be totally overwhelming. If however you have already taken care of your needs *before you go there,* the food is no longer of much interest. Really, with this simple strategy you make sitting down at a table full of food less challenging.

You can be calm when visiting with friends and family. Eat before you go out for *any meals* with anyone. It's so much easier to manage your food intake and stay in control.

We've actually been doing this thing backwards, trying to control food intake by not eating, misunderstanding this is going to create hyper vigilance and anxiety around food. We are indeed hungry and this reality will take over driving anxiety.

The better way is: eat first, and stay calm around food, even disinterested in the food that is there.

Another client was recovering very well from bulimia, and had met a new boyfriend. He invited her to the company Christmas Party. She'd been doing really well eating on her own, around him and in front of her family. However, when confronted with the thought of going to the Christmas Party she became somewhat overwhelmed and resorted to her old patterns of controlling food by restricting. There would be plenty of food and lots of new people she didn't know which triggered her restrict and control anxiety.

She resumed her old pattern deciding not to eat the whole day before going. When she got there she applied her usual heavy restriction pattern, no flexibility and rigid. Small salad, vegetables, a small piece of fruit, and then toughed it out while watching everyone else taste all the varieties of the bountiful Christmas Buffet.

The next day she was full on binging and panicking about weight gains. When we restrict we are almost punishing ourselves, and bulimia will fight back for control. It's better to eat before you go, and then eat normally at the buffet and resume your food patterns the next day. It took her a couple of days to balance back and thankfully it did not trigger purging again. This is a great place to apply the 80/20 perspective and let you try some foods and then back to your usual food intake the next day. (the 80/20 rule is in Challenge 3).

It's OK to eat before I go out for dinner

When we were little, we were told "don't eat before dinner, you will ruin your appetite" remember? *Yes, the family rules.* So we continue with some of these old rules. Eat before eating? *That sounds crazy won't I ruin my appetite? Won't I overeat and gain weight? Well you aren't three anymore, so I guess you can change your rules about when to eat pretty much any time you want to.*

Once you begin to retrain your body and mind by eating three small meals and three small snacks, you will find it's optimal if you take very specific care of your unique requirements around food. Food is fuel; "I need the fuel at the times of day that keep my body, brain and soul working at optimal capacity." If you find that you are out with others, they may not be as aware or balanced as you are around your food intake.

"I was at a BBQ at a friend's place; I was visiting her for the weekend. She had been very attentive to my needs around food and supportive of my recovery, however, once the party started and people started arriving and drinking and chatting, food was the last thing on anyone's mind. I found myself in the kitchen freaking out. It was now 9 pm and no sign of anyone interested in eating. I had no way out and simply had to wait.

At 11 pm her partner suddenly remembered to turn the BBQ on and start cooking. I was livid. I was so angry at them; I felt they had purposefully tried to sabotage my efforts. How could they do this to me?"

Once you take back control of the way you eat, you will never be in this place again; this woman learned to eat before any event, party, or even out for dinner at a restaurant; at her usual time, with a small meal, so she could be relaxed and calm around food. *This never happened to her again.*

If you are out with friends or family for dinner, or special events; this can be a very challenging time for anyone. Not only is there food involved, generally there are family members to deal with at these moments which creates excitement around the event itself. This is often where eating disorders really get started at these "safe but volatile" events. We all have families and family events with related stresses that happen; however, what you choose to do with the resulting feelings will determine a different behavior and outcome.

A safe strategy for any event is eat before you go, and be sure you have safe snacks with you, plan so you can slip away easily if things get too intense. "My mom always hangs onto me and I feel so guilty leaving, she's so unhappy in her life". Create a pre-agreed escape clause before you agree to attending. Just tell your family, "I'm coming however, please know I have to leave by this time, as I have…." and make that just as compelling or don't go. Then you have the option to stay longer, if things are smooth and easy. If it does get tense you have options.

One client I worked with had such a powerfully anchored command set up around attending to her mother's wishes. If her mother asked her to come, she would cancel everything to be there, even if the function was not in her best interest. "Your cousins are here, and your aunt is bringing all the food". Even if it was going to create more challenges for her, she would just cancel everything, and go. Later we realized the negative feelings programmed her internal strategy and would drive her bulimic behaviors, and could and did ignite a week long binge and purge fest.

Often a problem time for bulimic behavior is late evening into early morning. Many clients complain they can't fall asleep without doing bulimia first. Easy ways to shift this non-resourceful pattern is to finish eating all foods by 7pm in the evening, add in a light walk after dinner, and head to bed when you are sleepy instead of eating. Shut down computers and cell phones that are stimulating and instead read a book for a few minutes before bed. Dim lights, and take a warm bath. Use the MP3's provided with this material, and drift into a delicious deep sleep. Late eating stimulates the system and will keep your internal organs busy processing the foods. Use Dandelion supplements, or take as tea for a deep and restful sleep.

Second Position: An "Out of body experience"

Anxiety often shows up when we are unsure of ourselves, feeling as if everyone is watching us, judging us, and even staring at us. We begin to get those little panic feelings starting up the back and across the chest. Running for the hills feels like the only way out. The sounds around you begin to change, a little perspiration starts, you feel like you could pass out, your heart races, these are all signs of anxiety and you could *just jump right out of your skin.*

Often we do just that. When people are sensitive to these feelings they begin to anticipate more feelings like this and "get out of their body" before the event happens. It's as if you leave the body standing there watching the frozen you, in the moment.

Let's slow down and take this in another direction:

Pay attention to the fast speed which you float in and out of your body, what happens next? What do you think about, what do you see, are you comparing everything to the last time? The fear around recreating the past, when you passed out and had to be taken to the hospital, everyone thought you were going to die and you thought you did, heart racing, breathing rapid, blacking out*: it can be really scary.*

Remember that event now and see it through your own eyes, just run the movie past the end of that event, to where everything turned out okay and resumed normal again. You survived and you are indeed here reading this book, whew! Take a deep breath, and relax. Panic attacks are generally not life threatening. They are very uncomfortable and based on vignettes from a past experience with the majority of the intensity being focused on how to avoid it ever happening again. In a way, it's a form of protecting yourself from that kind of experience; however, it's now become an avoidance pattern and creates a distraction as you relive sequences and project negative future possibilities based on these past experiences.

Anxiety activates the adrenal response, *fight or flight* and when this fires off it shoots directly to the heart muscle bi-passing the brains reasoning centers. That's why you can't talk yourself out of the feeling. *I'm feeling this panic, I'm freaking out.* And it takes about 40-45 minutes to re-absorb the chemicals released from the body during a panic/anxiety event. It can feel awful.

Enter bulimia a solid "something to do" a pattern interruption during a feeling *I don't like.* Like any drug, I can make this feeling go away by going off somewhere and just binging and purging. This can last about the same amount of time. Bulimia often is a "go to" place to manage feelings, anxiety, and tension, feeling bored or just being restless and not knowing what to do next. Bulimia is the filler; the distraction to interrupt the "negative" feelings and negative self-talk, and it takes care of the incident long enough for you to forget about it. It's a clear strategy that has become integrated through the neuro-net and is the catch-all for every negative thought.

However, what if you did something completely different? What if you noticed the feeling, and then allowed it to remain. Feelings habituate, they start to move and then go back to the start again. What if you allowed the feeling, and observed as it moved. Then you could imagine the feeling running in the opposite direction. What does that feel like now?

How does one do that? Enter breathing

We just have forgotten to *breathe*. Deep slow breaths take us out of our thinking mind and back into our body. Focusing on your breath stops the thoughts as the mind becomes "mindful" of your breath. The reality is that there is nothing to fear, there's no big mountain lion facing you, it's just your friends. Breathe. Deep breathing calms and relaxes the body, clears the mind while rapid breathing can create a state of panic, intense anxiety or trigger a panic attack. It might seem everyone is watching you, and observing you, but more than likely they are aware of the intense energy you are sending out and everyone is wondering "what's wrong?" So then they ask and that often makes it worse.

You might think, "I noticed that girl is laughing and having so much fun, everyone is paying attention to her, not to me, and I feel like I'm not important to anyone". That feeling can feel like when you were at home with your family where you seemed to disappear into the walls and no one even noticed. They didn't seem to care so you did just that. Disappeared and ate, and threw up, purging the "bad" feelings along with all the food and drifted off in your own little world for a while.

What would it be like to just be with your feelings? Try it out and see what happens. Feelings are like waves; they come and go, they ebb and flow. They start in one place and move to another, what if you could get the feelings to move in the opposite direction? They are intense for a moment, and then disappear as you are trying to remember the feeling. As you send the feeling back in the other direction it actually changes the flow and shifts the feeling completely. Try this out, imagine that feeling of anxiety that rises from within you, where is it exactly? How is it moving, in what direction? What happens if you stop the movement and move it in the other direction?

Exercise: Collapsing a feeling

Find a feeling you don't like. Perhaps feelings of anxiety maybe you're late for work and can't find your car keys. Maybe it's anger, really angry with you for not remembering where those keys are. Go ahead see if you can find a similar situation like this and let the feeling intensify to 10 out of 10. Hear what you say to yourself, then telling your boss why you are late again, and see yourself searching madly through everything. Now follow the feeling, where does it start and following it through step by step to where it moves in your body.

It's OK to imagine little arrows on the feeling to show you how it's moving (like a flow chart). Imagine pushing the feeling outside of your body. Can you see it better? Is it still 10 out of 10? Good, now follow the feeling as it moves through and cycles back to the first place it started from. Repeat the sequence again and again. Just slow it down, and start it going in the other direction. Spin it and spin it over and over again and now move that whole image back inside your own body.

Keep spinning this feeling in this new direction, stronger, slowly at first and then faster and deeper in this way for about 15 minutes, really relax as you do this and go past the old feeling so it becomes neutral.

Try it on another feeling; maybe find a feeling which you would experience resentment when you are with your mom or dad. Perhaps a sister or brother; the more you practice with shifting these feelings the more you will come to know you don't need bulimia to distract you at all; you can do it this way. It takes far less time, and you won't waste a lot of money on the food either.

Exercise shifting anxiety around food and eating:

Find the feelings in your body. They are there and they trigger your reactions and responses. Let's see how this goes:

First, find a time when you were eating with the family, it might have been a time when everyone was aware of your behavior and they were just watching you eat, you could feel the tension mounting in the room. Imagine yourself in that place now, and take a moment and feel where you first felt the feeling in your body. Maybe it was in the gut, a feeling in the tummy?

Maybe it was in your head and moved to behind your neck or back?

Where does the feeling start?

The interesting thing about feelings is they move, like a wave, in a pattern. I want you to go back into that scene and feel how that feeling of anxiety moved in your body. Where did it move to?

Did it move back again? Is it going up or down, around in circles, squeezing or expanding? What is the feeling doing? Can you draw it in the air, or motion it in front of you?

How fast is it moving? Can you slow it down?

If you can slow the feeling down, then you can close your eyes and imagine where it's moving to. Just watch as it flows through your body. If it's helpful you can even ask the feeling to put arrows on it, and show you which way it's going.

Use your hands to motion the direction the feeling is going - Good.

Imagine pushing this feeling outside your body and watching it move, spin collapse, expand. Now because you can, direct it to stop and go in the other direction, that's right as it moves into the other direction watch it respond to your command.

Now while it's moving in the other direction, imagine pulling it back inside your body. Do this for at least fifteen minutes. The feeling will move through its cycle back to where it started, and then repeat the sequence again and again.

You are now in control of this feeling. Next time it starts you simply:

Become aware, what direction is it going, push the feeling outside, watch it moving, spin it in the other direction, draw it back into your body. And continue to breathe and spin the feeling in the opposite direction.

EXERCISE FOR THIS CHALLENGE: Eating Again: Food is Just Fuel

In this challenge, food becomes just fuel. Whatever the past events this challenge asks:

- Eat three small meals a day, proteins first, and three small protein rich snacks
- Eat before going out with friends
- Eat before any big family gatherings or events
- Make a list of your family rules around food

Changing the view of ourselves

There may be an old memory where people teased or said mean things about weight or size. Or a time when there was such anxiety around the fear of eating and fear about not stopping or having eaten too much and you may have felt rejected because of your size.

One client had a vivid memory of telling her dad she'd eaten too much. She said he didn't think there was anything wrong with it. She hadn't mentioned she'd thrown it all up afterward.

Because dad didn't think there was an issue with this behavior, she thought "OK with him, OK with me" and she continued.

Many clients go to their doctor with irritable bowel and other complaints and yet do not disclose to the physician the whole story. It's as if you expect the doctor to figure out what is wrong with you, while withholding a very crucial piece of the problem. Of course if you tell the doctor what you are doing they might recommend very different treatment. If the doctor doesn't ask, doesn't have time, doesn't catch on, it's like that dad that didn't pass the test his daughter put to him. Withholding vital information isn't going to help you, it can kill you.

The fear, anxiety and panic increases, so you don't tell the whole truth, you delete information and if they don't ask specifically… you distort the problems endeavoring to hide bulimia. And these behaviors continued over time and with intensity can kill.

Creating the new image

This time, let's do this differently: imagine the image now: is it vivid, a still picture of you, caught – suspended in time – suspended in the image, can you see yourself?

Notice how easy it is to fixate on one area of your body, let's pick the thighs. And now in your body, touch your thighs together, "they are touching": panic!

Allow this image to become a movie in your mind, when this was a very different feeling. A feeling of health not focused on your body at all. Feel what you felt, see what you were seeing, and experience how good you felt.

Now breathe in deeply and relax your body. Place that image of good health and feeling great about you over this panic image. Let the two merge into one. Let the feelings merge into one feeling, and let yourself step right into the one body now. The body of success and feel it.

You can defuse ridged stances by reframing them to work for you. "I can't do that" can change to: "I can do this if I simply change the way I see it, or hear it, and the way I think about it, which will change the way I feel about it."

Changing how we see things:

Next time you are out, pick up a large rock and place it sitting in the palm of your hand
Close your eyes, and imagine making it bigger, make it as big as the room you are sitting in
Now shrink it back down to its real size
Now, make it smaller, like a tiny pebble in your palm.
Open your eyes and look at the real size of the rock

Imagine food you usually can't resist
Bring it right there in front of you
Notice the size, is it moving or still?
Are all the colors present?

The more you look at this image, the more compelling it becomes, *I just have to have it now!*
Quickly drain all the color out of the image
Change it to black and white
Shrink it down to a tiny speck
How compelling it is now?

Good – now the next time you are thinking about those compelling foods, do this first:

Shrink that sugary carbohydrate food down to a speck
Flick it way into the distance
Bring the image back and it's getting bigger
It's changed, this time it's a protein shake
Or a hardboiled egg
A beautiful piece of salmon
Or any other high protein food that will give your body what it really needs

Keep practicing this exercise. The power is in the practice. Make a list of foods that stimulate those old behaviors and the healthy foods you would rather be eating. Do the exercise…

Eat the protein, leave the junk sugar behind

CHALLENGE 3:

TAKING BACK YOUR POWER

Through artistic expression and expansion we experience arts and talents in music and writing, acting and dance. We are creative energy expressing itself here on the material plane. This expressive energy seeds a desire for expansion and growth; however there is a need for balance and moderation, enabling a flowing energy that can allow the creative ability to express spontaneously. This is undermined by routine or time schedules and often is at odds with the rhythmic energy that desires to become the flow of life. Spontaneity and enthusiasm are keys to creative flow. There is a love of luxury with lots of joy and optimism; however, overindulgence has been dissipating your life flow and while friendly and creative talents are all necessary for the many interesting experiences the key here is balance in all things. Without it energies are scattered, lacking clear direction and focus. The key areas here; bringing balance into your life will allow your talents and gifts to really grow and flow.

Reframing "All or nothing thinking"

Re-balancing beliefs and allowing for "imperfection" actually takes us out of rule-bounded behavior we've been living with. Each day, more rules, "I'll do it perfectly today", then breaking that rule and destroying your self-esteem even more. Balance this with the 80/20 rule which allows for the small deviations and doesn't destroy your recovery with a simple miss-step. This challenge is to allow for 20% deviation from the "rules" each meal, each day, each week and each month.

OBJECTIONS:

I like a little crazy; I like it a little wild and out of control, I don't like boring

I like unpredictable and I like adventure and spontaneous excitement

I don't want to have more rules about food; I have had enough of them

I just want to eat normally, like everyone else

Life is not meant to be so black and white; in fact life has shades of gray and all the colors in between. We often get caught inside this frame, not knowing how to be, what to say, when to show up or how to act. This is how we get caught up in trying to be perfect, and setting up rules that become, *have to and must.*

"I'll behave this way, I'll weigh this much and no more, I'll only eat these foods, and nothing else. I can have my cake, eat it too and then just get rid of it, I win!"

These thoughts are often the constant companions of someone with bulimia, and they keep one stuck in the behaviors that are not resourceful. Further they just aren't true; these are generalizations that are anchored to patterns of behavior that keep you locked into bulimia. Let's look at how we can shift some of these thinking patterns into something that is more resourceful and useful in your recovery.

The 80/20 Rule: replaces those old rules and the *all or nothing thinking* restoring balance.

Moderation in all things means I'm not bound by any food rules and I am in control, I don't need to vomit food to control what I take in, or use laxatives or enemas to "get rid of it" either.

80% of the time, I follow three *small meals* a day; three *small snacks*; eating proteins first.

80% of the meal, 80% of the day, 80% of the week, 80% of the month, 80% of the weekends 80% of holidays, 80% of the year, and year after year, this is my way.

20% of these times, I have room for options. I can change a snack, or forget my lunch, or forget to pack what I wanted and even eat out as it comfortably fits into my 20% and doesn't trigger old "let's go crazy with food" behaviors.

I don't have to do it perfectly that was just a mind game I used to play with what was "good or bad" and coaching myself with having "blown my perfect streak, may as well go all the way and then vomit up the food". *Food is just fuel.*

20% of the meal, the snack, the day, the week the month, I am balanced, relaxed and moderate in my choices. There is no perfection around this behavior. No good or bad, it's the middle road, the middle way. Balanced. This is normal around food.

I can have the piece of cake and keep it too. It doesn't have to start a binge to purge; this is just part of the 20% and defeats the rule-bounded behaviors that entrain bulimia.

Panic doesn't ensue because a piece of chocolate got into my mouth or one more strawberry than I thought I would eat, or should eat or set as my limit.

What is normal?

Right now, you know your normal is not normal, the way you have been using food is not normal "food as fuel" consumption. Comparisons are redundant you can't know what that other person ate or didn't, and they can't know what you ate or did not. For a while you need a plan, so for these 90 days you need to restructure a plan that works for you. Then follow it, each day, moving through the process, one day at a time to create that balance and a new normal for you. It's important to know that when someone is observing or checking on your intake these are not really "safe people" to be around. They create fear and anxiety around food, and a feeling of being judged. It is much more helpful to know what is normal for you within yourself. *I know just what I'm doing and how to do it, I know who am I and I have room for this in my 20%.*

Sometimes the conversations about food and eating too much in our families have caused us to engage in these discussions. As we listen to our mothers' guilt about food or consumption or the never ending complaints about wanting to lose weight we can end up listening to conversations over and over again. The repeated conversations get embedded in our psyche as well. Maybe your mother never had weight issues, but wanted to protect her daughters from them through negative commands and restricting too. "Don't you think you have had enough of that? No you aren't hungry now, it's not time to eat, just have a piece of fruit and wait until dinner." These kinds of food compulsions are very negative installations and cause our daughters to stop listening to their own body endeavoring to please mom, or at least not draw any negative criticism from her.

People won't know about your 80/20 rule and it is so OK to share this with others to diminish their anxiety around food too. You would actually be helping them, as you help yourself normalize anxiety around food. "I have the 80/20 pattern I follow and it works for me, so I'm good with this."

Changing our inner rules for eating

Let's look back at the history of your food use:

- Often the foods were out of balance. There were too many junk sugars and preservatives, genetically modified foods - grown and prepared in countries far away from where you lived necessitating the use of junk sugar to preserve them.

- We may have been forced to punish our stomachs as children by eating foods at times and in amounts that someone else deemed right for us. No one listened to you that you were not hungry for that much food. No one heard you that you had just been eating half an hour ago and that your tummy was very small and already full
- You probably didn't have any choice in what was placed in front of you, as to its size, portion or nutrient value, and you simply had to eat it all, whether you wanted to or not
- Breakfast may have been nearly non-existent. These days everyone is on the go to get out of the house (a meal you could miss and no one really cared too much)
- Snacks are full of sugar; as are juice boxes and school catering has not solved the junk sugar issue either
- Lunch has no real protein; it's high in junk sugar, preservatives and nitrates in prepared foods
- The afternoon snack is often missed completely
- Arriving home you are ravenous, you eat a huge amount of food, then face the family drama at dinner. Dinner can be fast food or take out because everyone has a busy schedule

That was on a good day, if all the times for eating were appropriately observed. Generally each day we found ourselves in the "low fuel" position as we headed home after school and we could eat the house down we were so hungry. Often we did just that.

Food as reward system:

Delay the gratification and food becomes anything but fuel; the more you wait for dessert, a treat, or a celebration, the more excitement it builds. Once you get the food you have been waiting for, the chemistry in your brain releases a positive flood throughout the body and brain. This entrains restriction and binge eating patterns. The restricting drives the release of dopamine and endorphins and can make the mindless devouring of food a drive to ensure enough goes in to facilitate the vomiting portion of the program to get everything out. Eat six small protein rich meals each day and avoid these old traps.

Society's Use of Food:

It's the start of a relationship "let's have dinner". It's the basis for family celebrations, let's have a special dinner, let's go out for dinner, let's have a BBQ and get to know our neighbor's. It's appears at the end of a relationship too; let's eat ice cream, cookies and self-sooth our broken heart.

From birth to death everyone brings food. Food is the foundation of every relationship in our society and food is everywhere. From beginning to the end, we are all in a relationship with food. It is the fuel of life.

There is also a belief that some foods are good and some foods are bad for us. And it seems all the foods that taste great are bad. When we eat certain foods in certain combinations it can make us feel physically sick as well.

There are enough books written now and we do know when we eat a lot of sugar and wheat based carbohydrates, we're going to have problems with gaining weight. That is a given. Plus we now know these foods are so modified in their origins they have embedded pesticides right in the DNA of the seeds. Our bodies cannot easily process these toxins.

Fast foods and fried foods get associated with fun. Going to games, going to the fair, going to an outing even a "road trip" has fast foods associated with it as fun and excitement. Pizza is a party, but they are high in carbohydrates, contain the wrong fats and include "junk sugar".

This is generally 80-100% of a person's diet growing up in North America.

The fight for controlling food in the family starts first thing in the morning and doesn't end until last thing at night. Moderation is not observed by our parents or our extended families and often kids recognize when mom is eating chocolate she's a lot easier to get along with.

Food as fun! Food as a treat!

When we have a birthday we get *rewarded* with cake and ice cream. The cake and ice cream are the things that everyone is waiting for at the end of the party. In some families, any emotional outburst is rewarded with sugary foods. If there is an emotional crisis or a catastrophe, food is the first choice to heal the loss, wound or illness. Food is often used in our society as anything but fuel. It's used for celebrations, family gatherings, and excessive intake of food during these kinds of family gatherings is both "allowed and encouraged".

"You aren't eating all your dinner? What no desert? I made this especially for you, it's your favorite"

In addition, over the past 100 years, the majority of people have moved "off the land" and into cities doing jobs that leave us sitting behind desks. And we ride the bus, drive or get driven to our destinations.

Today we use food for more emotional needs than ever before. This lifestyle has led in general to less exercise. The result is the growing girth of the population and the children of today. Being the "big kid" at school was never OK and it's still not today. Being the skinny one isn't very OK either. As teenagers we are really fearful of "standing out" in any way. If we're different, we're going to get baited by others for it, from family members, parents, teachers, and peers too. We're already in the place where we hardly know ourselves. We're changing every day and now we have to worry about who is noticing or not noticing. Where we are different is just as important as where we are the same.

This pressure comes from all directions and we have nothing to defend ourselves with. We can feel isolated, alone and begin to attack ourselves with thoughts and internal dialogues that are often much worse than anything anyone else might say or even think about us.

What's up with sugar?

Scientists figured out how to split the sugar molecule somewhere in the 1940's. The glucose molecule has 12 carbons around the nucleus forming the whole molecule and our brain needs the whole glucose molecule to build and repair neuro pathways daily. As well, every cell in our body has requirements of "energy" for the same purpose. In creating this substance they called "Junk Sugar" they named it *fructose, dextrose, sucrose and high fructose corn syrup.*

Commerce recognized an industry value for this. It was cheap, 100 times sweeter than sugar, and as addictive as street heroin. It was used as preservatives for processed foods giving food a longer shelf life.

When you read your labels you will see these junk sugars seem to get into everything. And they don't provide the necessary *glucose* at all; that was changed in the processing stage. The sweetness spikes insulin and the brain needing the glucose for development, accepts this sugary substitute and it gets very hungry for it trying to use it for brain development. It is not the complete glucose molecule so it doesn't get the job done, and the brain keeps sending you a signal for more and more sugary foods. These sugars are very addictive especially to a child sized metabolism.

In fact the more you restrict and starve the body, the more images the brain sends you of increasingly sweeter foods. And it makes the images bigger and more enticing, because it is getting desperate for fuel and then you give what it really doesn't need; junk sugar.

Complete glucose can safely be found in fruit and some vegetables, however, it's the whole fruit and vegetable that holds the whole molecule. This is what your brain is really asking for.

We feed children sugar and it sends their already insulin sensitive bodies into the scream zone. (They are insulin sensitive because they are small people and a donut with high fructose levels will spike insulin very high and very quickly). Children don't know what's happening to them, they can't figure it out, and they slowly sink into the abyss of the insulin highs and lows. While parents say: "there must be something very wrong with our child" as they bounce around after eating sugary foods. Even natural sugars from fruit will spike a small body's insulin.

A mother called me from Ontario, complaining her six year old child would only eat McDonald's French fries and ice cream. That was their six year old child's daily intake of food. I asked the mother, how does she get these foods? We buy them for her, because she won't eat anything else. The mother said, her husband was furious with her too, and neither of them knew what to do.

It can be frightening for parents, if your child suddenly stops eating nutritional foods and starts eating from a very limited selection of poor quality foods. Parents don't know what to do, and everyone is challenging your parenting and offering advice.

I asked the mother, how long has this been going on? *She said since the child was three years old, but she always had problems eating and throwing up as an infant.* Both the parents were working so lots of eating out at different drive through restaurants. She and her husband were struggling and their marriage was in trouble.

We talked about preparing vegetables, fruits and good nutritional foods, but this woman had a million reasons why she didn't have time for this. She packed her daughter "healthy lunches" every day from a variety of pre-packaged cheese, peanut butter and cracker snack type lunches. Opening one of those high processed snacks after it's been in a lunch case from 8 am to 12 noon each day; the aroma must be anything but appealing. In order to eat these snacks they have to be cold enough to cover up the smell, and they are loaded with chemicals, preservatives and of course junk sugar. The child never opened these lunch packs.

Eat on your schedule not everyone else's

We start our lives with people feeding us every few hours, so we can live and thrive. By the time we start to understand language, we've already had food become the weapon we can submit to or use to control others. Parents plead, beg and create all kinds of games and crazy strategies to get their kids to eat the meals they have prepared for them. Children get this: *I can really wind my parents up with this.* Even the two year old knows feeding time can be a great opportunity to practice her resistance skills or polarity response.

The two year old may not know that these are polarity responses, but they know that when they behave this way mom gets really excited, and things start happening. Dad yells too, everyone gets dramatic and emotional. Wow, this is fun!

One young mother noticed immediately when her infant daughter was no longer interested in nursing and would just take her off the breast. She would wait a while and then feed when her daughter was hungry again. This followed into the toddler stage. She offered her food at six different times during the day, with breakfast being significant, then lunch and dinner too, while three other smaller snacks were offered in between. As soon as the child was finished with the food, no matter how much was left, it was removed. There was never an argument about eating. As I observed this young mother, she followed the same for herself. She would serve her meal, and eat some of it, however, she was often the last one finishing and she never finished everything on her plate. Slow eating, and always leaving some food behind. She never saved food, or retained left over foods from her plate either. For her that was garbage and she "let it go into the bin". Food was just fuel. If food did not get eaten or her child was not hungry at that meal, then she knew the toddler would be hungry at the next meal. She never turned to food or eating when she was upset either. Food was just fuel.

Food was neither a punishment nor a reward system

It was just fuel. She referenced her own body, and when she was full at a meal time, then that was her body's choice and she respected and honored that and stopped eating. Now interestingly enough, the dad in this family started to get involved as the children got older, and his view was he didn't want them turning out like his wife, throwing half her dinner away all the time. While his wife could defend herself, the children fell under his rules that if food was on your plate you should eat it all. There was a war on now.

It's interesting to observe as one parent is making dinner, and the other one is feeding the toddlers some sugary foods. Once sugar hits the stomach, it begins to ferment, and very quickly they are not hungry and wound up like tops. Dinner starts and the drama begins: *"Eat just a few peas, how about three bites of your meat, just drink your milk"* and on it goes with the child on the hot seat, when really the parents need to re-examine their strategy around food.

Food is fuel, it's just fuel.

It's not a negotiation, nor is it a time for war games or power struggles at the table. Some parents insist that all the food on the plate of the child must be eaten before they can leave the table.

However, the child did not select the size of plate, the portion size, nor did they have a say in what was prepared for dinner, or how it was prepared and yet here they are facing the firing squad for refusing the food. When parents force food issues it's generally about their personal agenda and often not in the children's best interest.

Kids will float through likes and dislikes about different foods with regularity

These mixed messages around food can create power struggles in families. Some foods represent sweets, treats and fun from one parent, while just an hour later kids are sent to their room for not eating their dinner by the other parent. Purely due to the fact the child's tummy had been sabotaged with sugary snacks beforehand. Parents don't like to be confronted on their behaviors: *"Oh come on, those donuts didn't create all this; she should have eaten her dinner"*.

Most people can recall at least one experience where they or someone in the family, were forced to sit at the table until the last pea was eaten. Usually if the parents are smart they won't reinforce this kind of power struggle, you won't win and ultimately will be dealing with a bigger issue when the child is old enough to resist. As parents it would be better to help children listen to their body and support them in good food choices and habits. Endeavor not to focus on body shape and size of others, or indulge in chatty gossip with your daughters when out. What you focus on your kids will too, and often they start the internal comparisons based on having overheard your comments about someone else.

"She should never wear those tights. Those boots make her thighs look huge." You might think these comments are lost on your daughters ears, but inside she's thinking "do I look like that?" Just don't start this with your kids, and if you slip and say something like this, then correct yourself, and admit:

"That wasn't a nice thing to say and I should not have commented on what someone else looks like, it's not a good practice to get into." Your kids will respect you more for your integrity and honesty, than the miss-step in an unconscious expression.

There are underlying belief strategies at work here. Let's look at them:

1: Parents have different approaches to food and eating
2: Some are comfortable respecting and listening to their body first
3: Some are not interested in power plays over food
4: Some will want to win no matter what - it's a game
5: Sometimes it's a drama /power struggle between the parents
6: The children get mixed messages about food and often pay the price
7: They also learn there are different rules for different parents and situations
8: They quickly learn to hide the fact that dad took them to the drive through and they all had fries and milk shakes after school and are now not interested in eating mom's dinner, and no one says why otherwise dad is in hot water and it won't get repeated

Secrets about food and self-indulgences start early

When families have issues with food these will very often transfer to the children. Oversize portions, eating at wrong times, eating in spite of having no real hunger or having eaten just before a scheduled family meal is not taken into consideration. Children are often forced to override their body signals and eat it all anyway. This doesn't even take into account the *big issue of sugar*. Some families feel sugar is out, and do not allow their children any sugar at all. When they come into school years, it's everywhere and kids will eventually get some sugar.

Let's be realistic and not set our kids up with unrealistic expectations and ultimate failure, all because we want them to follow our rules blindly. Most kids know who in the family has issues with food and how to push those buttons. Don't give kids these kinds of buttons, because when they are 15, you will be powerless to influence them differently. Make food fuel, *just fuel*.

Sugary substances shouldn't really be considered fuel. It's found in items we actually consider "real food". Macaroni and cheese dinners, hot dogs, ketchup, relish and mustard all contain sugar, to name a few. However, the food industry generally laces their products with junk sugar; you and your kids are addicted to these foods for this very reason.

One of my clients was the middle child of three. Her other siblings were boys. Every meal time, her mother served the dinner for the family in the dining room, while she ate in the kitchen. The father had full control over the eating at the table with no involvement from the mother. The children had to eat everything on their plates, and mom served the same amount for all three kids and dad. The boys had no real issue clearing their plates as they got older, however, she continued struggling to finish what was in front of her.

The argument with dad was not one worth having, as she was left a few times at the table for hours trying to finish up her meal. As she grew older she learned the best way to eat it all, was to eat it fast. The faster it went in, the more likely she could be done and gone. It became a race at the table to finish first, and she could eat the largest amount of food in the least amount of time, washing it down with her milk. Done... As the boys grew and gained weight, she grew and started to gain a lot of weight.

Meanwhile, mother in the kitchen also had an eating disorder. She would regularly polish off whatever was not eaten by the family in the kitchen while the family ate in the dining room then purge it right afterward.

The daughter's issue didn't come to light in the family until she was well into her late teens and by then she used everything to get the food out of her, including over use of laxatives. She was bulimic all through high school. Bulimia was the way to deal with her emotions, food and keeping her family at a distance. Her father was the one she tried hardest to please. He never suspected she had an eating disorder until she was into trouble with her bowel having to disclose her medical emergency to the family.

Shame, Guilt and Compulsive Lying

We might wonder: why "shame and guilt"? Why would you feel so shamed by this disorder? There's another aspect to this disorder and that is the idea of getting caught. Everyone noticed and envied your slim body and it seemed you could eat anything and not gain weight. You were envied. It can feel good to be envied by the family for your thinness. Sometimes that's the only thing that gets you attention. "I'm really good at being slim everyone wants to be like me."

Once everyone knows you are binging and throwing up it's all been a lie. No one believes you anymore, you've been caught "cheating". Discovery at this level is damaging to relationships with boyfriends, classmates and parents. It can be a very lonely and isolated life and there is nothing more terrifying than getting caught. Some will go to many extremes to ensure no one sees or knows what they are doing.

There is a sense of pride maintaining the facade for family and friends, loving that attention while knowing inside just what it costs you to achieve it.

"I grew up in an environment where it was difficult, but important, to gain approval. Now at 48, I really enjoy the envy of my friends, they all look at me as if I'm magical or something. I still wear the skinny tight jeans and latest fashions and I know I can look years younger and everyone envies my figure. I love it, they envy me and they just can't seem to look as good as I do. They don't know that I have to live this lie, hide my behavior, can't be in relationships. I live alone and have a very lonely life. My libido is zero; it's been gone for years, so while a relationship looks interesting I'm just not interested in sex enough to want a partner."

What can parents do at home?

De-escalate food dramas and anxious behavior around food. Create mealtimes that are quiet and peaceful. If both parents are fighting at dinner time how can anyone eat and digest their food? Put healthy food in front of your child. Let them pick at it, *and say nothing.* When dinner is over remove the foods and quietly proceed into the evening. Do not offer any other foods during the evening. Going to bed hungry one night is not going to kill your child and breakfast the next morning will look very different. It may take a week of persistence with this, but keep at it; you can change the food dramas much more easily than you have been telling yourself. Pack protein rich lunches and snacks and do not get side tracked or maneuvered into fast foods or take outs. Eat what you feed your child. Three small meals pay attention to portion sizes and do not engage in any coaxing or drama around food. Remove all that old worry energy and simply *expect* your child to eat. They will. Mirror neurons are active in each of your children until much older. If you sabotage your child with sugary foods, there is no one to point a finger at. Just stop doing it. Make food and meal times as part of the family health and wellness plan, instead of packing it with drama cycles. Eat together, and do not watch TV or work on the computer during dinner. Who are your kids copying most? It's you. If the parents are in discord, then make meal time a neutral zone, better yet, resolve your differences so it doesn't affect meal times.

Endeavor not to comment on each other's eating habits in front of the kids, just eat, enjoy your foods, and respect each other's choices and decisions around food. *Your children are always listening.*

Weight gains in North America

"I don't want to gain weight", is a great distraction that redirects us all to look in a different direction, rather than at the addictive behavior. It's a trance induction in itself. "I don't want to gain weight" takes us inward to our own belief patterns around suggested weight gains. *No one wants to gain weight.*

It's never a good thing to gain weight in the west. The testament to that is the number of diet books and videos, weight loss programs, exercise programs available in the multi-billion dollar business of dieting today, and most of us subscribe to it.

We are *panicked* in the west about weight gain. And that redirection works, because it helps everyone around the individual with bulimia go into their personal trance state and silently *we all agree as we are distracted by the obvious.* One father called me just before his daughter came to see me for the Bulimia Breakthrough three-day intensive and asked in a hushed and urgent voice: "your program won't make her gain weight will it? We wouldn't want that to happen to her."

The helping professional that tells the person with bulimic behaviors to "just eat normally", really loses credibility the moment that statement is out. The individual with bulimia knows instantly she's dealing with someone that doesn't know she can eat 3700 calories several times a day and vomits it all up because she would indeed gain weight. "Just eat normally" is very discouraging to hear because they don't have a reference for what normal is anymore. It was lost to them, long ago.

Three Small Meals a Day, Three Small Snacks, 80/20 Rule

There is nothing special going on with this eating plan; in fact it is the Diabetic or Glycemic Index eating plan: eating three small meals a day, protein rich and three protein rich snacks in between. You will feel better, sleep better, and have more access to your thoughts, feelings and emotions. You will have a new energy you have not had for a very long time.

It might be helpful to know the bloating and stomach issues during the "re-feeding" time will heal in about 6 months to a year; you just have to be patient with this. It eventually goes. Essentially bulimia has been driving your life since the first time you tried it. All control has been handed over and this is the way to get it back.

If you eat this way, bulimia will "stand down", you won't need it anymore it's really been trying to keep you alive, and keep you from starving yourself to death.

The 80/20 Rule does not mean:

I can go eat a lot of binge food now to reward myself for having been good all month.

(Well it's my 20% isn't it?) - No, it's not.

That's bulimic behavior. *Restrict and reward.*

The reward system of the brain wants a fix.

I've been at work all day; I need a reward, a treat.
I've been good all month, I want that reward now.
I haven't' used bulimia for a month, I deserve one now.

80/20 is the concept of re-balancing – I can eat a single chocolate and leave the rest, I can relax at a party where there are foods that are sugary.

I don't plan for, think, wonder, or daydream about a food. If it's presented and I eat one, I don't have to throw everything up and out of my body because I didn't follow my good and bad food rules. In fact, I don't judge food that way at all.

It doesn't mean because I ate some sugary foods, I should throw in the towel, eat my normal binge to "get rid of what I just ate" either.

I don't have to eat it all, and I don't dwell or fixate on the "go crazy opportunities" where I see them.

It also allows for the miss-steps; I ate too much at that dinner and had some cake too. It was in fact one meal out of a week of meals, I'm okay with this. I will keep it. 80/20 rule balances and allows for all things in moderation.

Obsessive Checking and Comparing

Complex Equivalence:

I feel my pants are too snug = "I'm checking I might have gained weight"

I saw that other girl and she looks so much thinner = "I feel fat"

I heard my mother say that all the women in our family have big butts =

"I will probably have a big butt like everyone else in my family"

How do we stop this kind of comparing? At the end of each statement above read in: **"so what"**.

Mastering the artful re-frame

Feeling: it's subjective, you might be feeling this and you might be wrong, and these jeans might have gotten into the dryer, or just out of the wash, *you could be wrong.* The three pounds up could be from eating salty foods and retaining water, or that you didn't drink enough water in the last 24 hours or the bloated face from cortisol production. This will disappear too. How can you re-frame these inner complex equivalences?

Notice the structure of your thinking, its generalized, and non-specific and it's a statement that triggers your addictive behaviors. Shift these kinds of statements by reframing the inner panicky thoughts:

So what, I'm not giving this anymore notice, I'm stopping this now

So what, I am not that girl and I don't want her life either, so I'm not comparing myself to her body

So what, just because some in our family are big, I don't have to do this and I won't

I feel healthy, I feel strong, and I know following my own path is right for me.

EXERCISE FOR THIS CHALLENGE:

Sometimes we hear things and then extrapolate what we "want to hear" or thought we heard, and then start applying that to the *whole of our existence. We distort the truth, delete aspects of the experience, generalize and even deny the real truth.*

Write out some areas in your life where balance is needed and applying this 80/20 rule might help you gain more control.

Some examples of all or nothing thinking you use:

If my weight goes up by 3 pounds, I'm sunk - I can't live with that I like to keep my skinny clothes around because they remind me of how far I have to go I will only eat at night, I'm saving myself through the day so when I start empty I know I can get it all out.

The basic steps for anchoring a positive resource

Remember a time when something amazing and wonderful happened to you, something that was so special and all about you. If you can't recall something initially, don't worry, just imagine what it would *be like* to have something wonderful and special happening to you right now.

See yourself as if you are right there experiencing the whole thing. What would you feel like? What would you say to yourself? Can you make the image a moving picture, life size and you are in your favorite colors beaming a wonderful great smile. Now choose a word that might represent this experience for you, add a touch by pressing your thumb and finger together; be certain you can repeat it easily.

We are constantly experiencing anchors in our life. Smells, sights, sounds, taste, when all our senses are activated strongly this is the peak of the state itself. Right in that moment, take a deep breath, feel amazing and press the finger and thumb together while repeating your special word(s) in your mind.

Great work! Now take a break and think about something rather neutral to you. Like the weather outside right now. Good! Notice how you feel, just neutral.

Now, test the anchor you just set by squeezing the thumb and finger together again. Notice the changes in how you feel, breathe deeply, observe it in full color, expand that feeling. If you can, put yourself so fully back into the memory, feel everything you felt, everything you heard, smelt, sensed, and then increase it with taking a deep breath in and expand that feeling through your whole body.

Now, squeeze the thumb and finger together and let this feeling become a new powerful state for you. While you squeeze the thumb and finger let a colour come to your mind and think of your word. Use these all as "anchors" to help you return to this state easily.

You could add to this wonderful state that anytime you see this colour, you have imagined in your mind, you will also slip back into this wonderful state of calm and peace. In this way your deep self will continue to "practice" this state for you, so it's something you don't have to do consciously. And you can do this with the word or phrase you chose too.

Repeat these feelings, sensations, thoughts, and images, make them big, full color and be right there in the moment, until you discover feeling the same experience. Take that deep breath in, and squeeze the finger and thumb together. Imagine stepping right into that image in your mind, and be in your body experiencing that experience. Press the finger and thumb together again. Now, do this at least 10 times intensifying the feelings. Stop, clear your mind, now press your thumb and finger together, release all the images, the sounds but keep the feelings. Do this at least 10 times.

Test this by returning to a neutral thought, like the weather. Feel as you return to a normal state and now press the finger and thumb together again. Feel that rush of positive energy again and breathe deeply into it, bring it into your body. Using it when you are a little bored or when you feel a little anxious creating a positive helpful resource state that you can use anytime, anywhere.

The more you use a positive anchor, the better it works for you, the more lively excitement and graphic detail you put in, the more it increases the response and intensity. Spend some minutes setting up this powerful new anchor. We're going to use it lots!

CHALLENGE 4:

CHOP WOOD, CARRY WATER

Dr. Donald Hebb (Canadian Neuro Scientist in brain plasticity) first coined the phrase, that "neurons that fire together wire together" and program your brain through habituation, ritual and compulsive behavior. In other words, what you do over and over, entrains the brain into repetitive patterns. The brain likes to find ways to automate and habituate process. Make it faster; make it "mindless" so we don't have to think about it, we just do it. Just like we did in the last exercise, you can program your brain and set up little inner signals for your brain to automate these good feelings for you.

For example: Do you still have to think about how to tie your shoe laces, or how to ride a bike? No, the brain already learned that and it's wired the connections deep into your subconscious. Just slide into your shoes and your fingers are already reaching for the laces. Make a move to get on a bike and your body is already managing the complex set of skills to navigate, propel, balance, steer and with resulting joy in the effort. Our brain doesn't register good or bad judgments; it merely takes pleasure in repetitive processes and if repeated often enough it will automate them.

Once the automated process is in place, we'll have to do something completely different to change and rewire that old program. It might sound daunting as we consider how long it took you to automate shoe laces and riding a bike, but not really, because your brain has its wonderful internal chemistry to help make challenges exciting, enjoyable and rewards this with a flood of those feel good chemicals. The more challenging a task the greater the reward… it just feels so good to achieve something you have been working at for a long while. A complicated dance step, a challenging exam, finishing a race, or completing any task that's been outstanding for a while… *it feels so good*!

We can notice a significant measurement of brain entrainment when we notice the amount of "boredom" you have to fill in your life. The more boredom, the greater these habituated behaviors have taken over. No new skills, nothing much going on, and your brain dislikes this repetitive patterning and will seek all kinds of distracting behaviors. Your brain is a powerful tool, creative enough to replicate function outside of itself. It's so powerful we don't yet understand all the brain's capacity for change and learning. It's almost magical how the closer we get to understanding the brain the more it surprises us with new potential. I sometimes wonder that our brain is not both fully co-creating our potential and also providing us the limitations and blocks we set up to keep ourselves from moving too quickly. Like a masterful computer, more powerful than anything we've ever created so far, the brain continues to grow, expand and show us our unlimited potential. We are indeed masters of our own personal universe and we endeavor to keep it in tack day to day. If Stephen Hawkins has a brain that can think and process the way his does, and we all have a brain similar to his, then is it our limiting thoughts that keep us entrained to what we believe daily?

Our brain accepts our stories, no matter how painful, sad, limiting or depleting they are and it will help us stay that course by repeating behaviors to match our restricting and limiting thinking. NLP helps us make these changes quickly because the brain loves the game of learning new things, it's always up for it!

One client had a fear driven belief that there were two months of every year when things were the worst for her, and the rest of the year she had to dig herself out of the disaster of those two months. The first month the behaviors were the worst, and she visualized all the past years in those months, and focused on them, and repeated the stories over and over to others. The images and the experiences began to replicate into the same month, in a different year. And this happened year after year. She was on her fifth year of this very same experience and was terrified this would be the same disaster.

This time, what we did was shift the patterns with a very simple phrase: "I just don't have time for this, this year." And then we added "I'm asking for this to be the best month of the year for me this year, right now."

Seriously within days everything started changing and shifting around, her calendar filled up, she had NO TIME for the old behaviors. Before she knew it she was eating on her schedule daily, forgetting about food, because she really needed the fuel to keep up to her incredible schedule!

She said to me "I don't know what happened but I'm eating regularly, I feel great and I'm so happy"

She had changed her story and changed her behaviors, which reinforced the new story, and her brain loved that she was now mindfully aware of all it was co-creating with her. Her universe was giving her exactly what she wanted. Magic!

Time to change entrained patterns and this takes steady repeating what we do want and letting go of what we know is no longer of any importance to us. We simply "chop wood, carry water" and we *just do it. (thank you Nike!)* Day by day, bit by bit, we change old patterns through interrupting the ones we don't want, and repeat consistently stepping into the change we do want. The brain quickly begins to automate the new behaviors; *in fact it's faster than you think.*

How does this affect my thinking?

We are chemical in nature

Dr. Eric Braverman, M.D. in his book: <u>The Edge Effect</u> offers some real clues to what has been happening in your life with the addiction of bulimia. When behavior causes the distortion of our internal chemistry these depletions show up as "triggers":

GABA, Serotonin and Dopamine in deficient levels interrupt your self-control; rob you of necessary sleep, creating depressed states which push the body to get carbohydrates and sugars for energy and function.

Neurons that wire together fire together. The synaptic connections of these habituated behaviors connect and fire off a chemical reward system that is so compelling you will compromise anything to get the fix your brain wants.

The mechanism of delivery is to restrict foods until your brain experiences starvation signals from the overall system. Now the entrainment of behavior as odd as it seems to others is firing off on multiple levels of the system and this behavior is entrained below consciousness. This is why you can't control it, make nice with it, or survive it. The only way to undo this pattern of behavior is to feed the body and avoid the starvation triggers. In this way you have regained control at the conscious level.

There are days when you make up your mind to get control of things, and just power over the binge and purge cycle. However, go back to any aspect of the behavior and it's as if the pattern was never interrupted at all. The brain doesn't forget it retains patterns for future use. That's habituation. Like learning to tie your shoe laces or ride a bike, the brain extrapolates the patterns and retains the information below consciousness so you don't have to think about it, or remember each step of the complex process. It's doing it all for you. The more complex and involved the various sensory levels, the deeper the levels these behaviors wire together.

Here NLP and Hypnosis help us re-pattern and interrupt old habits we no longer want. Working at the deepest levels of the brain (the subconscious) we re-pattern behaviors that no longer serve us.

Those old compulsions seem to disappear. Once they are interrupted we no longer reach for them as the first choice during stress, boredom or uncertainty. Instead we begin to build new resources through more meaningful connections. The brain does it all for you. It's not your enemy; it is in service to you. Comparative analysis is how it learns new patterns; this not that, this red one, not this blue one, tie the shoe laces this way, not that way. As you instruct it to carry out these tasks you are entraining the patterns and it does it for you, mindlessly, effortlessly.

Pretend you don't know how to tie your shoe laces anymore. Then go ahead and pull your shoes on, you are tying those laces before you even think about it.

Retraining the brain; however, is often easier than you think. You might after the fact, remember, "Hey I didn't even think about going for a binge and purge, even though I was really upset about what just happened". Instead you opted for interrupting the old pattern and finding new resources and facilitating new outcomes which reinforce the new patterns.

One client that felt really challenged about making these changes suddenly saw things going in a different direction and not from a conscious level within her:

"...things have never been better. It's been two weeks since I have last engaged in my eating disorder and I feel like a completely different person. I am even letting myself go out on dates with someone I recently started seeing. It's crazy. I don't have any urges to engage or anything and I am really not sure why. I love it!"

Notice the new story! Your brain likes to learn new things. It gives the brain pleasure to learn and create new synaptic connections. It helps the brain stay young to learn new things and helps the brain expand and grow. Learning new things delights the brain, and it reflects this delight by flooding the system with those feel good chemicals and hormones.

Change builds new synaptic connections
that wire together and will continue to fire together.

The more obvious enjoyment we are experiencing and reflecting back to ourselves as this client did, the more the brain will continue to fire off those new pathways. "This is what I want." Now it's easy to adjust and tweak these new behaviors to get the optimum results for you.

With a little time, practice and persistence, choosing the new behavior instead of giving into the old entrained patterns you will master this too. Your brain is fast, it's quicker than you think, and it will program your new patterns for you in seconds, once they are in place, then choice keeps them there. Revert to those old patterns and it can feel like you have lost ground. Instead of lamenting the loss or failure, just go back to the patterns you do want and your brain will continue to reinforce it.

During the first few weeks of any recovery plan you however, must remain vigilant. Opting for a day of free-for-all food and you will find yourself in trouble again. The key here is often you judge the process, "this didn't work for me". It did, you just needed more time to continue to reinforce the new behavior. Remember the old behaviors had years of reinforcement, entrenched throughout the whole of your experience. This new pattern won't need much; however, it will need your conscious commitment to keep on keeping on in the first weeks. This is the component of Practice. Like tying the shoes and riding the bike. It took some practice until you were even dreaming about it as a kid.

Chop wood, Carry water: one new thing and your brain is growing, do one thing differently in the moment and you break the old pattern. Do just one thing differently. Eat every day and you will have changed the core synaptic connection that triggers the binging and purging.

Choose the new pattern you want, not the old one because it's easier

How does this all get started for most?

Clients have shared they first decided to try bulimia in their school years, for most that is the starting point of their life with an eating disorder. They noticed others had tried this and it seemed like it worked. Innocently enough they reached out for something to help themselves feel better, feel like they belonged. Often they admired the person they copied. (Replicated, matched and mirrored behaviors until they automated it) Remember those first times? Pretty nasty and yet your deep self remembers the exact first time you tried and then forced yourself to keep at it. And the truth is, if you had known it would lead to brain entrainment and a heavy addiction, similar to any drug, most likely you would have found something else to do instead.

And just because a coach or trainer, an instructor or teacher suggested you follow their behaviors you know you would not have done this if they suggested drugs, cigarettes or alcohol. It's just that *this* seemed dramatic, exciting and like it made you part of an inner secret society and no one said "this is an addiction like any other drug – you won't be able to stop."

Anorexic behavior or severe restricting seemed like a good idea to control weight gains which are constantly fluctuating during the teen years. We learn about it from books, hearing others talk about it, or even from movies; information on *how to* is available everywhere today. A friend might have even suggested it. I've had clients share their dance instructor suggested "why don't you throw it up like the rest of us".

One day, out of frustration, fear and panic, realizing you had just eaten about half the kitchen after school, you raced for the bathroom and threw it all up. *"Hey this works, I can eat as much as I want and then just throw it up and I won't gain weight".* This new behavior generated a positive result. *Here's something I can use to control my weight. I can restrict like crazy, lose all the weight I want, and then binge whenever I feel like it too.* The weight loss generated positive attention from parents, teachers and kids at school too. People noticed and that felt pretty great too. Going back to the old weight was not an option. "Wow, you really lost a lot of weight this summer". And the fear of weight gain now becomes a dominant *anchor* in the pattern of bulimia, supporting your continued use. In fact bulimia doesn't work as a long term weight loss solution, eventually it stops weight loss.

The downside: "Once you start, you cannot stop."

What defines Addiction? It's a state of being enslaved to a habit or practice or to something that is psychologically or physically habit-forming, to such an extent that its cessation causes severe trauma. Any use of a substance or behavior that is compulsive and is damaging to your body, mind and spirit; destroying relationships with others and especially compromising your relationship with yourself. That's addiction. Here we have now lost the "choice point" and are enslaved to the behaviors. It's no longer an option, it rules your life, and runs it too.

Bulimic behavior is compulsive, damaging and out of control

Doing this for days, weeks, months and years, has contributed to the escalation of addictive behaviors and substances. So it's no longer about will power or shaming yourself for your "weakness" it's now a comfort, a reassurance, a mindless gorging which when released, gives you a chemical high equal to using cocaine. Through the use of bulimia, the patterns entrain the brain and you use it for every life experience: good, bad or indifferent, bulimia is always there for you.

To change this we stop using it for every life experience. We develop new synaptic connections in the brain associated with new experience. Even in stressful moments or moments when we are without constant activity, when we are feeling a little mundane or bored, we don't give in to the old way.

Ending the war within

The strategy for maintaining a certain weight offers a sense of comfort. Emotions get attached to bulimia, and coping or working through life challenges have been handled by bulimia. Bulimia, in fact, any addiction robs you of developing critical life coping strategies by distracting, isolating and comforting yourself with the addictive behaviors instead.

Bulimia acts as a reward system, with big payoffs: "I've been good for several days, and Friday night is available I plan to really treat myself". The suggestions you give yourself and the restricting behavior all drive the reward patterns. The reward for being so good all week while intensively restricting increase the chemical release during the binge and purge and increases the "High" afterward.

The Addictive High

A side effect to vomiting after the binge is the "addictive high". This is often not shared, nor even understood by the person using bulimia, but it is there just the same. If they don't like how they feel, or a sensation in their body, it triggers negative thoughts, and a planned binge and purge. Anxiety, tension, fear, a little anger, a little jealousy, a little envy, never ending boredom and the drive for binging and purging become the exit strategy used to get out of the negative emotional feelings. Bulimia takes a good 40-45 minutes to distract the emotions and secure the high with food and vomiting.

And we don't stop here, make that a celebration, fun, a great time with others – home and celebrate with a binge and purge as a "treat for myself". Self-pleasuring with bulimia is often lost on most, but not the person choosing the behavior. Bulimia solves and resolves everything.

More than anything else, it can terrify a person considering letting go of bulimia. "How will I manage my state when I'm upset, when I'm fearful, when I'm anxious? Bulimia handles all that for me now. Bulimia is my best friend; at least it's always there for me".

Generating a "high" after binging and purging, releases the *feel good cocktail* into the blood stream propelled through excessive releases of insulin, endorphins and dopamine driven by the excitement of restricting, rewarding then purging the food from your system. GABA is depleted entraining impulses and compulsive behavior, which release a host of other 'chemicals'. Like a huge hit of any drug it satisfies the pleasure centers of the brain in seconds and that high lasts about 40-45 minutes. By now the issue has passed, the argument is over, the disagreement with mom, the fight with the boyfriend, the impatience with your boss, the celebration, the successful interview, all forgotten for the next 40-45 minutes.

And it's the same high every time

Many people with bulimia have never tried any other addictive substances. These are often the "good kids" the ones that cause no problems at all. The ones that did well in school were great at sports, and teachers loved them. Drugs: no way; smoking: never; drinking, no; and they don't recognize they are into an addictive pattern they cannot get free of just like any *street drug.*

<u>A simple definition of addiction:</u>

Any use of a substance or behavior that is compulsive in that you cannot control or stop yourself and is damaging to your body, mind and spirit.

Other addictive Substances:

Alcohol and drugs can be used for the same purpose. When you have one addition it can be a slippery slope into other addictive substances. Clients have often shared the use of other opiates have stopped bulimia for them for a time. The problem is the underlying issues have still not been addressed and using any drug to self-pleasure and avoid life is going to continue the problems, and won't solve bulimia. In fact it will just make it harder as you have added more addictive substances to your life.

Delaying Emotional Growth:

When we use a drug to alter our experiences in life, we stop our emotional maturity. We don't develop the necessary coping skills in our teenage years. Instead bulimia seems easier and helps avoid all conflict, tension, worry or discomfort. Boring Saturdays, long weekends, Friday nights, anything where time is unstructured and the idea of self-pleasuring through binging and purging becomes the focus.

Planning increases the reward system:

How can I get my fix? What will I get? I'll be at home and I don't have anything to do on Saturday either so I can just laze about and maybe finish off what is left over. Critical planning starts and will be executed with excited precision. Bulimia entrains a pattern of "pain and conflict avoidance". It handles everything which can result in isolation and low levels of depression.

The lying, sometimes stealing, the waste and the behavior all generate shame and guilt

This is detrimental to your self-esteem and self-worth; as critical self-care seems unimportant – you feel you aren't worth fighting for.

➢ "I feel so guilty, because of all my bad behavior" however, if you stop the behavior, then the avoidance of life still remains as an entrained pattern, "*Oh, I just don't like to bother people, I don't want to worry them; I don't want to say no, because someone could be upset with me. I'm the one always helping others, it's how I value in myself*".

Avoiding anything to do with confrontation, feeling sad, angry, even boredom; "*I hate it. I don't want to be upset, I don't want people to know what upsets me, and I don't want anyone to know they can upset me. I don't want to feel anger, or emotions, and bulimia takes care of all that for me.*"

Hiding behind being perfect yet underneath it sits these toxic beliefs that keep you in a prison only you have the key to.

➢ "*If I speak up, what will everyone think of me? What if I don't speak right? What if they judge me? I don't feel safe asking for what I want or need. I hate to confront others. I never win an argument, I get confused, I forget my argument and I just end up hating myself even more. I sound stupid, I don't like myself, I sound*

> *like I'm complaining. People will judge me; think I'm
> a nerd or something."*

Fears of being seen, or heard; self-judgment and any comments from others now feel like an assault across the already heavy negative belief strategy you use daily.

> ➤ One client shared she had challenges at work. The owner was away for a few weeks and an assistant was put in charge of the rest of the employees. The assistant relished the power and started directing and criticizing everything. This continued for a few days, until my client was choking on her anger and outrage. She couldn't think of anything else but this woman's behavior and how unfair it was to everyone. The idea of speaking to this assistant was so intimidating it nearly caused a relapse into bulimic behavior, however, working it through: What's the worst thing that could happen? Can you really see yourself waiting until the owner gets back? What will you do then? Will you do anything about the situation? What is happening at work now? How do you feel about going to work tomorrow and experiencing this every day until your boss gets back?
> ➤ She said she was going to hand in her resignation. Quitting was better than dealing with the situation. Instead of doing that, we worked through the anger, and re-framed the situation in her mind. In this state she was able to figure out, that if she was going to quit anyway, why not tell her manager exactly why?

➢ It seemed reasonable, she had nothing to lose, so she went in the next morning, and told the assistant she was resigning and why. She said the assistant paled and had to sit down saying: "please don't quit, I'm so sorry, I just wanted everything to be perfect while the owner was away. She'll kill me if you quit, you are her best employee, you work harder than everyone and she really values you, please don't do this."

When we are teens and have to confront someone, we've often botched it up. *We're supposed to.* That is our trial and error time. It's time to experiment, with what works, and what doesn't. When we miss this in our teens, we have to play catch up and finally master the risk taking needed to grow emotionally. It can be really scary when you are in your 40's and still don't know how to say no or ask for what you want.

Delayed emotional growth

When we used bulimia through these years, we didn't develop the experience and maturity to take forward into our adult lives. Instead we drugged ourselves with food addictions and pretended it didn't matter. Problem solving seems too overwhelming. We don't know what to do, or how to do it, so we pretend everything is OK, and retreat into denial and avoidance. As we mature we continue isolating as it still seems easier than trying to figure out what to do about a difficult boss, not getting recognized on a project, or lying to your boyfriend as you prefer to spend Friday night alone with your addiction.

Using bulimia we can miss out on experiences that would allow us to speak our truth and stop avoiding our real feelings. Happiness is an inside job and it's not up to you to take care of others happiness or calm their stress or tension. Often that creates anxiety, simply trying to do the impossible. Letting bulimia handle stress for you robs you of a solid footing here. Often there is frustration and anger trying to figure your way out of something as avoiding what seems challenging just seems so much easier. Bulimia handles it all as you retreat from conflict and avoid painful situations.

Bulimia is an addiction and you have learned how to restrict and use food, in the right way and volume to produce enough insulin, and propel your own "feel good chemical cocktail" through massive releases of chemicals inducing a physical "high" and then numbing out for hours after wards.

Lying as a bi-product of bulimia and eating disorders:

What is not telling the truth?
Avoiding relaying all the information, remaining silent, sharing just a little to redirect the conversation?
When do you overtly lie to others to get out of a situation?
What if it's to get what you want?
Perhaps to get money for binging and purging?

How practiced are you? How long have you been doing
this?

If you don't lie what happens to you? Do you feel you
reveal too much, others will judge me? I won't have
control? I don't want them to know that much about
me? Do you feel like you are on the stand and only
answering the direct question?

Do you get a small sense of pleasure out of lying to
people and watching them accept your lie?

How do you build trust with yourself and others if you
don't tell the truth?

**To correct these behaviors we have to bring to
consciousness they are not good behaviors to have and
in fact continue to feed the lies to yourself about what
you are doing daily. When you lie to yourself the bigger
damage is your deeper self is always listening and it
knows exactly what the truth really is. This is how you
fragment trust with yourself and deeply wound your
relationship with yourself.**

Start by taking small steps to stand in your truth. Honestly
what's the worst that can happen? Someone says no to you?
You don't get what you want in the moment?

Life is here to engage with, participate in and co-create
with. In fact it's the most exciting journey when you start
asking clearly for what you want, and it starts coming to you
faster than you could ever have imagined and in the most
incredible ways! Life is exciting, fun and challenging. It's not
supposed to be safe, controlled and manipulated. Risking

and taking risks with the whole of your being, is just the most empowering thing you will ever experience!

Accepting at times, the co-creative aspect of your reality might know you need to take this step over *here,* I know it seems like it's a side-step, but when you do this, something is going to open up over here... Trust is part of finding new ways to solve your problems and disappointments in life. Start here and begin today to only tell the truth. As you begin this new behavior with yourself, you will find you no longer want to lie to yourself either. Very soon these changes will expand into your life so as you are truthful with yourself, you find you are with others too and on a much bigger scale than living the lies and distortions of an eating disorder.

Stand in your truth and you will see a massive shift in your life. You don't have to be "nice" to everyone hoping they will like you. You don't have to have the dramatic story of the week. You can just be in your truth. From here new things begin to happen:

- Self-respect
- Personal integrity
- Honoring yourself
- Asking and speaking up for what you want
- Self-trust
- Transparency
- Acceptance of others and yourself
- Feeling good about yourself – not based on others approval

- Disrupting the guilt and shame at a core level so bulimia *really makes no sense*
- In fact it's just a waste of time

Your Smart System

When you are restricting and vomiting or eliminating through excessive exercise, laxatives or enema's you are placing your body into starvation mode. Like a switch that goes on, triggered by the brain the internal smart system will optimize systems to maximize absorption and reduce all other expenditures of energy. In fact, your smart system will actually redirect resources for survival and will begin to store fat and consume muscle for food.

The body/mind connection is part of the smart system, when you force external changes to the system, the system will respond by making further changes to ensure its survival. You actually begin working against yourself. You are triggering chemical changes in a system that already knows just what it's supposed to be doing. Those changes trigger behaviors at the blood chemistry level.

- Cellular reconstruction is put on hold… prematurely aging your body
- Neuro transmitters and synaptic connections become entrained
- Restriction of nutrients holds the brain to basic survival behaviors
- Feeling isolated, fearful, unnecessary emotional fears and worries

- Isolation, foggy thinking and a constant sense of anxiety
- Emotional development is arrested to the age you started bulimia

Many bulimic clients believe that their own personal research into food is sufficient; however they don't have the whole picture. Systems in the body are not insular from each other. It's a problem with our view of the body. We compartmentalize the systems and treat them as if they are separate from the whole. But every system is connected and influences our body holistically.

Your brain is very complex and while you might keep telling yourself you don't want to get "fat", what your brain is actually doing: "store the fat and consume muscles for fuel." New synaptic connections are sacrificed, focus and attention are unimportant, memory useless, and survival is now everything. Reproductive systems are not essential to someone that is in survival mode.

Healing is compromised; the digestive track extracts nutrients every inch of the way. Your focus has been to get food out as fast as it goes in. So the digestive track itself is damaged, and unable to secure the nutrients needed to repair it. Often the biggest complaint is the pain, the distention or swelling of the abdomen and lower bowel.

Your conscious mind cannot direct the chemical changes and the variances in the cells of your body; you don't know how to do that consciously. Deep sleep is elusive when using bulimia and the night time patterns of binging and purging leave one exhausted and frail in the day time hours. There is a minimum ability to concentrate or cope; life is just draining and irritating.

During sleep our resources are put to good use restoring the body's internal organs. Here the liver, spleen, bowel, heart, lungs, kidneys, adrenal glands, gall bladder, all begin the restorative process. When we don't sleep, we become depleted and often exhaustion is mistaken for hunger.

Optimal Self Care and Self Love:

Your smart system has much more going on than you are aware of. Your brain masters the chemistry needed for your body throughout the whole of your life. It directs and redirects systems as needed. For instance, when you started restricting foods your brain knew your body would not be able to sustain a pregnancy to completion, so it took all your reproductive systems "off line". Your monthly cycle stops producing the egg and so the monthly release of menses is also stopped. This also compromises other areas of your system too. Your brain is also redirecting what it knows is essential to its sustainability and had begun redirecting all fat to storage during starvation. It also directed the body to begin to consume the muscles of your body for fuel. The intense restricting in anorexic behavior starves your body and your brain. The smart system below your conscious awareness goes to work to maintain what it can to survive.

Bulimia is running the smart survival system. As you opt for binging and then purging, some of that food is retained and it allows your body to continue to survive, however, not optimally as you are still in survival mode. That survival mode is powerful; it will shut down many other systems before it lets your body die. It robs systems to support necessary functions in the brain. Muscle is consumed for energy while it stores fat for brain function.

Thinking is distorted and you don't have energy to do things. Your smart system is conserving energy. You don't need to think to stay alive; you don't need access to memories, so your short term memory is interrupted and you forget things. It's the survival system that keeps entrained on food.

There are times when you feel like you are witness to some monster that has taken over your body and you are helpless to stop it. The survival system is so powerful; it is what has kept the species evolving for hundreds of thousands of years. You can't control this part of your brain. When survival mode is on it thinks of little else except food and where to get it.

Your smart system is working to keep you alive and when you come to terms with this and start working with your body again now the war between your head and you will be over.

EXERCISE FOR THIS CHALLENGE: Perceptual Positions - emotional growth and wellness starts with being able to step back, consider and make some new choices

1st position: Self, through my own eyes – here I feel it all; I have access to my entire sensory input, total self-reference (taking it personally)

2nd position: Through the eyes of another person – (overview of the whole situation)

3rd position: See yourself and other person in the situation – (observing both – more neutrality)

4th position: Universal view of the whole situation – (from the perspective of the whole experience)

Think of a time when you felt overwhelmed and frustrated with a person or situation – remember it vividly as you do this:

Position 1: See this experience through your own eyes, as if it's happening to you right now

Notice what am I feeling now? What do I see, what do I hear?

What am I saying to myself about this situation?

Step out of first position into a neutral position

Position 2: Imagine floating into the other person in the situation and looking at yourself, through their eyes

Notice what am I feeling now? What do I see, what do I hear?

What am I saying to myself about this situation?

Step out of second position into a neutral position

Position 3: Imagine moving to a third position where you can see yourself and the other person in the situation, just like watching a movie, notice your feelings.

When you think about this situation now, what do you notice, has anything changed? Take a moment and write your experiences here:

> I felt,
> I noticed,
> My body experiences,
> My thoughts,

Position 4: Universal overview of this experience expands your awareness, allows for heart centered, relaxed awareness. This is the "watcher self" aware and open to receiving input from the vast expanded mind, helping us in the moment. You can even access information here from a vastly expanded consciousness.

A good place to use this skill is when before you shop and shop only from your list, you can place yourself in this third or even forth position, so the shopping doesn't influence you at all.

Moving from where we are feeling and sensing everything to a place of observing from a different perspective and each one offers a different perspective on what is going on. This is you remaining in yourself, while trying out different positions, from associated – through your own eyes, to disassociated; through a part of yourself we can call the "watcher-self". Here you can take the time to consider all the facts and make some new choices.

It's a good idea to take a few minutes a day to practice this. Placing yourself in the third position, where you don't feel, you just observe. Once you have done this a few times, set an anchor on the third position, then if you are feeling overwhelmed at another time, you can quickly shift to another position.

Recall the anchor you set earlier squeeze your finger and thumb together when you are in the calmer watcher position. Use that great state to help you build this new resourceful state.

Practice that feeling (squeezing thumb and finger) so you can instantly get into this state.

From the watcher-self position, you can check and see if you are feeling tired, worried, or perhaps a little hungry? Here you might notice you have actually picked up someone else's feelings – check are these really your feelings? No not mine.

Great benefits of learning the flexibility of perceptual positions:

1: You have learned a useful new skill and expanded your awareness

2: You have a new perception to identify if the feelings are yours, or someone else's

3: You can slow the process down giving yourself time to think about things

4: You don't need to project anything negative on another person; or yourself either

5: You can experience zero anxiety, frustration, tension and you can resume your tasks

CHALLENGE 5:

MINDFUL MEDITATION

Now... silence lets the one behind your eyes talk...
— Rumi

Challenge five resonates with freedom and change and is the pivotal point between the first and the ninth challenge. It represents a variety of experiences through your developed five senses. You see, feel and hear there are so many opportunities for new decisions and direction in your life, but how? How do I get there? Overfilling your life with constant activity and curiosity becomes self-sabotaging itself: knowing the vitality and energy of life is alive in every cell of your body and that all your desires can come to fruition helps you make steady progress in the direction of regaining your health and wellness.

Some considerations for this challenge:

It is in your nature to avoid routine or confinement
Do you have an insatiable curiosity about life?
A love of pleasure - and self-pleasuring, which can lead to
    over- indulgences & extravagances
And then a deep despair and regret - manifesting as shame
    and guilt for having wanted it all,

A great compulsion for constant change and a drive for
    excitement
Routine and dull monotony feels like death to one's spirit

Change is the only permanence we know. Without change
we feel a sense of stagnation a feeling of being stuck. There is a
deep driving need to experience physical, mental, emotional,
and spiritual change that bubbly witty, enthusiastic and
active mind is always creating and striving for more.

Some have shared you are a natural entertainer, and this
often gives way to "center stage" and loving that excitement
and attention from others. The excitement is as compelling
as the experience itself.

The outer world personality is haunted by the introvert
within that often second guesses and fears the unknown,
berates, judges and restricts in punitive and painful ways.
Attachments to persons, places or things feel like dead
weight - the thought of a "day job" is agonizing. We can
find ourselves in transition from one moment to another
with everything hitting maximums in mood swings - from
excitement to depths of despair and back again.

This lack of balance can secure the diagnosis of bi-polar
and put you on medication, however, a way to re-balance
your enthusiasm for life and all its wonders is to embrace
"meditation". As this becomes a new path in your life, you
secure a greater command of your own mind, thoughts and
expressions of your life purpose. That might sound like a
life-sentence too, almost worse than taking medication: *A*

routine, daily, no change, dull and boring - isn't that "death" to me?

In challenge five we recognize we need to cultivate patience, and tolerance – as those old behaviors are often impatient. While there is a need for more variety and excitement you are not afraid of trying the new and different. Others may view your life style as bohemian, wild and carefree. Here you may find yourself up against your mothers views on this more often than you want to be too. A challenge here is to accept and appreciate each other just as you are, and let your differences become that which you celebrate in each other.

In Challenge Five, we learn to keep balanced, know what is harmful to your sensitive nature and simply do not indulge in it. Establish a belief system through attaining balance by choosing the middle path between extremes.

A ZEN staying: "let go...or be dragged"

Thinking fast, speaking fast, walking fast, moving fast, fast-fast-fast, everything is fast. How quickly can I get it done? How fast can I eat all this? How unconscious can I be when I'm doing this? It's an entrainment from days of bulimia. Sometimes we learned it as children, "finish all your dinner or you can't leave the table".

This challenge is to eat slowly... breathing and relaxing... placing small portions in your mouth, putting your fork down between bites and slowing the food consumption down. If you are eating a sandwich then putting it down while you chew your food. When twenty minutes have passed put the food away. Leave it for another time, or throw it away if that makes it easier to forget about it. Dispose of it into the garbage can (if you are still thinking about it douse it with vinegar or soap so you are completely done with it).

What are your strategies around eating fast?

Eat fast because it's too much and I have to get it all in there or I can't leave the table
Eat fast so I can get enough in to make the vomiting work
Eat fast so I can get it all out
Eat it fast so it comes up fast, or I miss the high and I won't be able to sleep
Getting a "high feeling" equals teaching your brain this complex addictive habituated pattern.

The key now is to slow down consumption; so it takes you the longest time to eat the smallest amount of food. Imagine saying that right now, "it takes me the longest time to eat the smallest amount of food". Now go ahead and read it out loud to yourself in your usual voice. Write it down here, in your hand writing, and when you have done this read your written note, back to yourself; out loud this is your new way to eat... *the longest time to eat the smallest amount of food.* At the end of 20 minutes I am done eating, and put the balance of the food away, or dispose of it in the trash.

When a person eats slowly they give the brain time to catch up to the tummy. They eat slowly and often leave portions on their plate when they are done eating. They don't feel compelled to "eat everything on their plate". They know their own portion sizes and they know how much they can eat and how long it will take them to do it.

They eat for about twenty minutes with pauses between mouthfuls putting their fork down, taking a rest and then they just stop, they are full. They listen to their body and that's all they eat. Even if it's delicious, they put it away, and eat it later. Haven't you often asked yourself how some people can eat anything and they never seem to gain weight? They seem to have no off limit, or bad foods either. They eat what they like and feel good about it too. To you this seems like "normal eating". Not everyone eats this way, sadly many have been convinced out of listening to their body and eat at wrong times, wrong amounts and wrong food choices too.

For you however, you are not eating at all, using heavy restricting to drive the chemical release when you binge, and then vomit. Purging until you have released all of what you consumed. This is nowhere close to any kind of normal eating.

Eat less, eat often, and eat slowly

It seems logical and reasonable that not eating would cause you to lose weight. Eventually however, it doesn't work as your smart system takes over and triggers survival mode. Now you are *Chasing Hunger,* you can't win at this, because you don't know all the things your brain is doing to keep you alive. Your brain is your best friend, it's been working at keeping you safe your whole life, and it's working very hard right now to keep you alive given the challenging circumstances its facing daily.

<u>A suggestion:</u>

My brain is my best friend; it's here to serve me
It's not my enemy it never was
I know it's trying to help me every day and in every way
I'm ready to listen to the deepest part of me, it's always there
     supporting me and helping me
It's not the other things I've sometimes heard myself say
I know the difference, those other things are not supportive,
     they don't help me, and I don't need to listen to those
     thoughts anymore, they are just thoughts and I don't
     have to act on them

_____

_____

_____

Chewing food thoroughly takes time. It also brings the tummy and brain into the dual awareness that food is being consumed. People who eat this way are the last ones to leave the table, they take a long time to decide what they will eat, and how they will eat it, considering every aspect of the food they will eat, and these people are often considered "fussy eaters". They can drive waiters and family members mad waiting on their demands for food to be delivered exactly as they ordered it. When it arrives, they look at the whole meal before them, and often declare "I'll never be able to finish all this food." Usually they don't. Usually they eat about a third of it, put their utensils down, check how they are feeling, and then try a few more bites, but generally, that's it. They are done. Once they stop eating, that's it.

They listen to their body telling them they have eaten enough and they are sensitive to what they are eating. Their eyes register the large quantity and even before they start they are already declaring they can't and won't eat it all.

Recovery doesn't hinge on this behavior, recovery will happen as a bi-product of it.

Calming the mind, releasing anxiety; how does meditation and mindfulness help us?

"Mindful Meditation"

In the west there has been a lot of skepticism about meditation. Interestingly both science and medicine have associated it with a "religious practice" like prayer, *so it must be the same.* And strangely enough religions hold the same view about meditation. "Its new age, we don't know what it is; it might not be good for you. We just don't know. We do know it's not religious and it's certainly not prayer."

As neither religion nor science will endorse it, meditation must forever stand on its own merits. Let's find out what science has discovered about meditation recently:

Dr. Herbert Benson first coined the term "The Relaxation Response" as a fourth brain state. This Harvard University professor found something in the brain he called a fourth state of consciousness, and we all have it – all sentient beings have it – because we all have a brain.

It's the brain's own system of "recharging itself". Every 90 - 100 minutes the brain does a little mini-shutdown and restart. It allows for information that has accumulated to be delivered throughout the brain and allows the brain to "rest and reset" and prepare for receiving information during the next 90 – 100 minutes. When we don't get these little shut downs other things start to happen in the brain.

Multi-tasking, no rest, interrupted sleep, exhaustion of a new baby, a new job, a move, all cause the brain to move into this state of actually "screaming" for this fourth brain state. Relaxation. Continue any one of these scenario's for any period of time and the brain begins to do its own kind of "forced" shut down. It's termed "depression". The brain begins to move down, as does our gaze, self-ward, inward. The brain needs downtime to restore and reset.

When you are new parents and sleep is just not possible, meditation for 20 minutes each day can restore you and give you added resiliency during these first months. For students studying long hours, adding meditation to your daily studies actually allows the brain to absorb more information and store it for later access as well. When recovering from extended illness and sleep is disrupted, meditation is a practice that is literally lifesaving. Meditation allows us to slip below the sensory gate, where pain is registered, and can often relieve pain for hours following. Meditation equates to about 4 hours of sleep, so the brain and body can restore and feel rested when sleep has been interrupted. Use it for jet lag, 10 minutes of meditation for every hour in the air, and you will arrive rested and ready to go.

There are so many benefits to meditation we do know about, what we don't fully grasp is the obvious benefit to stabilizing the brain chemistry and reversing unnecessary fears and anxiety. The anxious behaviors, thoughts and troubled choices continue to heighten and increase the problems.

It clearly helps us be better equipped to deal with life on a day to day basis where the mundane exists. Meditation can move those inner doldrums through releasing our own internal feel good chemistry

In Dr. Benson's book, The Relaxation Response, written in 1974, his extensive studies in this area essentially defined the relaxation response as your personal ability to encourage your body to release chemicals and brain signals that allow the muscles and organs of the body to slow down while allowing an increase of blood flow to the brain and allow it to recharge. It is now used to help people in a wide variety of stress induced illness, pain, and even recovering from heart attack. Allowing the brain to down regulate the stress hormones it moves us from "fight or flight - anxiety and panic" to calm. The measurable responses include: reducing blood pressure, and a heart rate. The Relaxation Response is essentially the opposite from the flight or fight response and it counteracts the physiological effects of stress. The brilliance of your own body to allow two very different and diverse systems: One - the sympathetic nervous system and the second the para-sympathetic nervous system, and when one is engaged, the other is not.

The fight or flight stress response occurs naturally when we perceive that we are under attack, there is indeed imminent danger present, *can you see that tiger in the corner?* This excited state is designed to protect us from bodily harm, help us fight or run away. Our sympathetic nervous system becomes immediately engaged in creating a number of physiological changes: increased metabolism, blood pressure, heart and breathing rate, dilation of pupils, and constriction of blood vessels all that work to enable us to fight or run from that tiger. What if there isn't a tiger it's just dinner with the family?

And yes, that can be a very frightening and life threatening challenge at times too, perhaps for some worse than the tiger; however, you can still manage your state better. When you feel yourself going into stress states of anxiety, tension, panic or unnecessary fear, knowing how to reverse this quickly is a god-send, and you can do it consciously with intention. In other words you don't have to sit there and "hope" this feeling will pass. You can actually do something about it, and right now and it doesn't mean you have to swallow a pill either.

Most pharmacies have a place where you can measure your own blood pressure. Next time you see one of these units, go ahead and check your own blood pressure. Sit in the seat, insert your arm into the sleeve, and then hold your breath for a few moments. Then breathe really rapidly like when you are excited, then hold your breathe again. Check your blood pressure.

Now, take your arm out of the sleeve, take three long slow deep indrawn breaths, relax your whole body, all the muscles, ballooning out the belly with your breath, (this is yogic breathing) and then slowly exhale. Do three more, and feel your body relaxing. Now measure your blood pressure again. Check the difference. It's impressive. Just in minutes all that anxiety is gone, just by breathing three deep breaths and slow releasing it.

Bulimia challenges the brain by stripping it of essential amino acids, hormones and neuro transmitters that build synaptic links in the brain; and seriously interrupts restorative sleep which prohibits the neuro transmitters from their essential repair time. It increases the loss of Serotonin through daily vomiting and lack of sleep, and the overuse of junk sugars strip away the impulse control centers. The brain is going through some rough times here and it's struggling to manage a system that is daily going out of balance.

Well, the good news is, in addition to being able to take supplements to help your brain restore, improve sleep and help those control centers of your brain, meditation assists in repair and restoration of neuro transmitters. It increases dopamine uptake, and releases endorphins. All part of your own "feel good chemistry". And you can do this for yourself every day. It's so much easier than you think to manage your own internal state. The high stress, adrenaline rush bulimia generates takes the body and brain into the opposite fight or flight response, generating adrenaline burn out and then activating the reward centers producing the "high" after vomiting. Meditation activates the opposite "relaxation response" and you won't abuse your body or your brain, in fact you are doing something very positive and helpful for all your systems.

Meditation and deep trance states allows the body and brain to work in greater harmony; these are some of the benefits you can measure:

- ➤ Finding things that used to "push your buttons"; a new calmness prevails
- ➤ Experiencing more confidence and greater sense of self-worth
- ➤ Relationships with others are more harmonious and hold less friction
- ➤ You feel happier, for no reason and even moments of "joy" slip in now and again

- ➤ Sleep is better as Serotonin & endorphins are by-products of meditation
- ➤ Physiologically, meditation reduces blood pressure, heart rates and respiratory rates
- ➤ Meditation increases the endorphins released into the blood stream, releasing the body's own natural opiates
- ➤ You will recover faster from anxious moments and adrenaline rushes. Meditation increases the brain connections between the left and right hemisphere. Thereby increasing memory access, recall, and strengthening the brains ability to work more efficiently
- ➤ Cellular restructuring and replicating is influenced through the neuro net or neuro highways of the body. The cellular receptors begin to crave these powerful natural opiates increasing receptors in the cells and meditation done at the same time every day becomes a delicious restorative time for you
- ➤ You'll accomplish all these things by just being in the "quiet mind" for twenty minutes a day. You'll learn to recognize unhelpful patterns of thought, feelings and emotions that tend to make your life more difficult than it needs to be. Meditation will help you choose new responses instead of old reactions
- ➤ Calming your mind naturally leads to greater empathy for others and through that: greater patience and empathy for oneself. All this utilizing your own internal pharmacy, *something you were actually born with*

➢ When we practice meditation daily, we begin to diminish the panic states by reinforcing the states of calm relaxation. It allows us a greater response time to stress, and in fact begins to down regulate the stress hormones. This brings a reduction in your heart rate, breathing rates and in general moving you into the "relaxation response" on a daily basis, assisting your body in reaching a new balance. You will always have the ability to *fight or flight* as needed, but you don't need that feeling just because you are going out with friends for dinner.

Is meditation for me?

You may be wondering whether you're "cut out for it". I hear a lot of people saying things like, "Oh, I could never meditate; I'm too easily distracted". Be reassured, anyone can meditate, and you don't need any special abilities to include this in your life. If you have a brain, you already have access to the relaxation response. Some of the behaviors around bulimia have increased the stress hormones in your body and brain which leads you to believe you just can't sit still or have a quiet mind.

The idea behind meditating is not that we're seeking to have "perfect meditations" or *zero the thought factory*. The point of a meditation practice is the "practice". What you do is to start from where you are and develop a practice that is just right for you. It won't be the same every time either; however, the more you practice the more consistency you will achieve in your meditation. A "practice" by name means that it is not goal oriented; it's something we do every day. There is no end to a meditation practice; it becomes part of our lives and there is certainly no perfection associated with meditation. It's a practice.

Meditation helps us to become aware of the habitual tendencies that are distractions in our everyday world. It also helps us to work with them as they become less prominent and we become less distracted, less anxious, more accepting.

And just like any program we start, we don't want to suddenly leap into it and expect 'perfection'. As a matter of fact perfection and meditation are about as far apart as oil and water.

In meditation we change gradually. Breath by breath, meditation by meditation, day by day, the change happens within our hearts and minds. Changes accumulate over time. It's possible to change from being a very anxious person to a very confident person; to move from being habitually in a bad mood to being more laid-back. We just have to practice.

The Brain on Meditation:

Even as little as ten minutes of meditation every day will make a noticeable difference in your life.

Meditation allows the body and brain to work in greater harmony and these are some of the great benefits of meditation:

Because meditation is a natural state of mind, it is not unlike a state of deep relaxation that you experience before sleep and when first waking up in the morning.

Meditation happens when brain waves are oscillating between the alpha and theta range which occurs between 4-12 HZ cycles per second. These states are called Ultradian Rhythms and anyone with brain function (all sentient beings) has this ability to "on – off" the brain for short intervals to allow for optimum or improved function.

Meditation and hypnosis follow similar patterns; with hypnosis or guided visualization you are agreeing to allow another individual to guide you into a deeper state of consciousness. These methods work quite quickly. The same optimum states of brain wave function are experienced during hypnosis which is also restful and very relaxing as well as a great way to let your own deep inner mind correct unnecessary or unwanted patterns of behavior that are no longer serving you.

Guided visualizations and self-help recordings are very helpful as you start bringing this into your daily life while you help your brain in recovery from bulimia with the restful relaxation response.

Many people describe their experience differently so there is no set standard for what you will experience when you are in a meditative or hypnotic trance. Some describe a feeling of lightness like floating, others report feeling heavy, and some report a euphoric sensation, almost like being intoxicated but without any negative side effects. Some people even report feeling nothing unusual at all, but achieve the relaxation response none the less. Whatever you experience please know that it's not a static experience and from meditation to meditation, hypnosis session to hypnosis session it can be different.

Every person has their own way of representing internal sensations and your day to day experiences are meant to be unique to you.

You can see why it's really useless to endeavor to compare your experience to someone else's. It's really about finding the right approach for you. Meditation is a practice, not a goal, an end game or something to perfect. It is a practice and one you can include in your life every day.

Some signs and symptoms of inner peace:

A tendency to think and act spontaneously rather than on fears based on past experiences
An unmistakable ability to enjoy each moment
No interest in judging other people
No interest in judging self
No interest in comparing myself to others
Less desire to interpret the actions of others
No interest in conflict
A loss of the ability to worry *(this is a very serious symptom)*
Frequent overwhelming episodes of appreciation
Contented feelings of connectedness with others and nature
Frequent attacks of smiling

An increasing tendency to let things happen rather than
make them happen

An increased susceptibility to the love extended by others as
well as the uncontrollable urge to extend it back

*WARNING: If you have some or all of the above symptoms,
please be advised that your condition of inner peace may be
so far advanced as to not be reversible. If you are exposed to
anyone exhibiting any of these symptoms, remain exposed at
your own risk.*

EXERCISES FOR THIS CHALLENGE:

Some mindful suggestions for you to practice:

- It is best not to eat mindlessly in front of the TV,
computer, or while driving the car
- Instead: set the table, have all the food you are going
to eat in front of you
- Look at everything there before you, appreciate the
food you are about to eat
- Eat for just 20 minutes, slowly, chewing and
enjoying the food, put your fork down between bites
and let yourself have time to chew and appreciate
the flavors. At the end of 20 minutes or if your body
feels comfortably satisfied before, push the plate
away, and clean up you are done for that meal.

MEDITATION CHALLENGE

For the next 90 days, you can access meditation and self-help MP3's from my web sites www.chasinghunger.com and www.waysofthewisewoman.com There are many great resources that will help you include this valuable tool on your journey to recovery.

You can listen to the recordings before you go to sleep at night. Many people find this really helpful for deep sleep. You can use them during the day as well. You may find that joining a meditation group could be very helpful, and yoga classes offer a form of meditation through body movement.

CAUTION: Please do not use MP3's or meditation CD's when driving the car or doing anything that requires your full attention. These MP3s are designed to help you relax your focus and rest your mind.

A basic meditation practice: Start by picking a time each day that works for you, same time every day and the morning is best:

- Find a comfortable place that you enjoy in your house where you won't be interrupted, place your phone on silent, or unplug it, turn it off and ensure you won't be disturbed for the next 20 minutes by family members, pets etc.
- You can place some items that are important to you here if you like perhaps a shell, or crystal, a candle to light, (and this isn't necessary to do either – I

meditate on the subway daily and don't have any of these things with me); I do however, have a place at home I have set up for meditation too

- Light your candle and sit back in a comfortable position
- You can sit on the floor if you like, use a meditation cushion, it's also very grounding
- If you sit in a chair, be sure your feet are on the floor and your back upright resting your hands on your knees
- With your eyes closed breathe in through your nose, and follow the air as it enters your body
- Hold this breath a moment before you exhale
- Now follow the breath out of the body
- Relax your body, from the top of the head, down to the tips of your toes, imagine every muscle is warm, smooth and softening; lengthening and softening more with every breath
- Repeat
- When thoughts come up, just bring your attention to them, imagine them in a bubble and let them float off - relax the tongue muscles - let it sink into the floor of your mouth, this stops internal thoughts from rolling around in the head
- Return to your breathing, *in drawn breath, then exhale*
- And repeat
- Each breath becomes more and more delicious as you focus on it and hold it just for a moment before you release it

- Now notice the space between the in drawn breath and the exhale
- Float into the space while continuing to observe the in drawn breath and the exhale
- Imagine relaxing all the muscle groups in your body from your head to your toes
- Breathe into the muscles and relax them, tighten them and then release them
- Breathe deeply and now as you have completely relaxed the body return to your breath, in and out, soft and listen to the sound of your breathing on the inside
- Do not concern yourself with the "level" of meditation, or whether or not you can keep thoughts from floating in or out, these kinds of thoughts can be distracting and often sabotage your efforts; essentially they are *normal*
- Mindful of your breath, simple meditation, do this for 20 minutes every morning and every evening at approximately the same times each day for the first month. Then miss a few days and see what you notice - it's really amazing!
- There are many methods of "meditation" and when you are just starting out I recommend you consider using the MP3's- they are "guided visualizations" and will help you attain a good level of daily meditation until you feel comfortable trying it on your own
- Some will say: this is not meditation however, if you are relaxing your mind and achieving this comfortable state daily, then indeed you are

meditating and your brain is utilizing the "relaxation response". Meditation is a practice, that means you do it every day and there is no perfect here, only the state itself is the gift to the one that humbly continues the practice

The Advances of Science, Medicine and Religion:

• Meditation was clearly refuted and disowned by Science, Medicine and Religion; however, with the recent studies in science and the softening of religion all these institutions are beginning to recognize while neither own meditation, it is indeed something we all do naturally. *It's just a relaxation response, with intentionally induced and derived benefits.*

CHALLENGE 6:

RE-FEEDING STAGES AND
YOUR WELLNESS PLAN

NOTES FROM OTHERS HELP ILLUMINATE THIS CHALLENGE

"I am still in a lot of gastric distress, the gas and cramping, nausea worsened, yet am doing my best with activities and sleep; getting enough nutrition, community acupuncture. I started taking a sub-lingual Melatonin added to the dandelion at night which helps me to sleep. I pray my gut starts to release as the nausea is intense and gas, like a fermentation tank. I am including magnesium. Vitamin c., chlorophyll, Cell Food, hot water bottle for cramps at night

I forgot to mention I drink herb tea, water, throughout the day, have a protein drink and tea latte before bed to hydrate. It really helps to know you have successfully treated women who have been very symptomatic for 20 years plus. Most people would just see it as insanity, beyond reproach and un-treatable. I appreciate your confidence and support in the challenge ahead. I feel a subtle opening starting to reconnect to that sense of bewilderment and curiosity as a child, seeing with fresh yet familiar eyes. I feel it is due to the commitment I am making with you so thanks for this gift of learning and opportunity to grow..."

We are focused now on feeding the body. *"Chasing Hunger"* is finished. Maintaining the 3 small meals and three small snacks daily provide nutrients and stabilizes insulin. The tummy is really never empty or starving, and it's never registering that feeling of full, bloated or overfull either. Between food intakes however, until the bowel and body adjust, there are going to be a few areas you have to get through. *This too will pass.*

Here are a few suggestions that may help your body regulate and re-balance during the re-feeding stage of the 90 day challenge:

- If you eat within 30 minutes of rising in the day, your body will set its metabolic rate for the day. Intake should include proteins and carbohydrates, and if you are Vegan, or Vegetarian, then adjust accordingly. You know how to do that.
- Generally if you can avoid soya as soya is primarily a product that is 98% genetically modified in the USA & Canada, and stimulates estrogen imbalance. As our governments have not yet asked companies to declare genetically modified foods so these are best to avoid. Soya Sauce is fermented and therefore does not have the same issues, however most soya sauces have wheat; and the wheat is genetically modified.
- Almond Milk is a good substitute however; it has very little calcium so it's important that calcium

is taken in through veggies, like broccoli and in supplement form (calcium and magnesium). For oils recommending coconut oil or oil from nut and seed sources, and Omega 3 & 6.

- Fish is a good option. Eggs are a great source of protein and free run eggs are available in most supermarkets today. You can keep hard boiled eggs in the fridge ready should you need a quick protein fix and there is nothing else prepared.
- Smoothies are quick, nutritious and easy to add in protein powders
- Use grains and seeds: quinoa/oats/flax/nuts/seeds/flax/pumpkin seeds

All in small sized servings, small bowl, small spoon etc.
The size of the palm of your hand is the protein serving
The size of one hand cupped is the size for cooked carbohydrates/ veggies/rice
The size of two hands cupped is the size for salad/veggies

Eating this way balances your insulin levels while eliminating sugar and wheat and will really speed the recovery of the gut. Expect it will take about a week or two of challenges, and then smoothing out over the balance of the 90 days steadily improving.

The gut is very forgiving, and even though it's had lots of abuse over the years, please know:

The digestive track replaces cells daily, so if we maintain some healthy behaviors for these 90 days, the gut lining will recover. This will improve once the behavior has been stopped, just give it time and refrain from "helping" through restricting or over use of laxatives. Let your body recover and it will begin to take back its daily tasks.

Go slowly as you add in other food groups and raw foods "see what happens". When you do this make sure your body is responding well in all areas. Only add one food change at a time. This way you have solid evidence of what is troubling you, what is healing and what your bowel can tolerate.

Optimum elimination is 1-2 times a day. Generally bladder elimination should be 4-6 times a day. The more fiber the more water you need to take in.

To ease constipation increase your water intake, while refraining from sugar, alcohol and juices for now. To assist the bowel, add Vitamins B, C and Acidophilus, also add magnesium before bed. (You can get your magnesium from an Epsom salts bath, just soak in a bath for 20 minutes, with a cup of Epsom salts dissolved in the bath water, it is absorbed straight through your skin).

Lack of sleep seriously affects elimination and can contribute to constipation. All those late nights binging and purging have been doubling down on the bowel, this will take a little time, however, be patient and persistent with this. If you start loading in chemicals and forcing your body to work you are once again engaging in the bulimic behaviors of trying to control the body.

Chemicals force your body to do what it does un-naturally. Instead, just wait through these first weeks. I know it's challenging but you can do it.

Some additional benefits as you go forward: your face will no longer be swollen and puffy, the dark circles will clear and your skin will look better. This is because liver function is improving and the kidneys are working better. You are healing. You will notice your memory is improving as is your ability to tolerate unpredictable events. You will even begin to notice on a daily basis, you aren't thinking about food all the time. This is your brain relaxing and shifting out of survival mode.

When we are on a healing path like this, we often focus on what is not right, what is not working. However, when we look at how much has improved it's really amazing how fast your brain and body can move back to health and wellness, back into balance. Within the 90 days your monthly cycle will stabilize, another solid indicator optimum health is returning.

Mood swings are less frequent, and in general feeling alive again, every day. Some clients have reflected back saying they can't believe they were living the way they were, it was barely existence.

Now as this is underway use a few supplements to assist your body back into balance and enjoy improved brain function, which helps with those "impulses". Use evening primrose for hair, nails and easing your monthly cycle. Use the MP3's and meditation daily.

Now: you need to move your body. Not too much either, just a little every day. A 20 minute walk after dinner each night will also curb those night time munchies. The body just doesn't want food right after exercise, and this will also deal with insulin uptake following the evening meal.

Exercise improves so many things:

If you move your body a few times a day, for short bursts of cardio, your overall health will be better.

Here's why: When we have short bursts of cardio exercise in the day, it increases our metabolism and it provides the uptake necessary for the insulin spikes. Eating between 7 am and 7 pm daily allows your entire food intake during the hours of the day your body and brain require the "fuel" and allows for the long fast each night allowing for the "repair cycle" through our sleep time.

Note: During this period of re-feeding and re-balancing the body, clients have shared that they have experienced nightmarish, panic dreams of binging and purging. If this occurs, it's a solid affirmation that the brain is clearing out the old files through dream time. *It's actually a good thing.* It often happens with clients that quit smoking or stop drinking alcohol or taking drugs. It is part of the clearing mechanism of the deep unconscious to do this during dream time breaking these old links, once and for all. The dreams seem vivid and startling and we can awake feeling like we had actually done the behaviors again. *But it was just a dream.*

Suggestions:

Disown the disorder: Please stop talking about this disorder as if you own it by using the phrase "my Ed, or My Eating disorder. This starts out as a bit of a habit, but it is saying something deep to your psyche and belief system. The psyche hears this is "ours" we own it, it belongs to me. Disown the disorder with changing "my" to "the". Just notice how often you phrase it this way and change it. "My Ed becomes, The Eating Disorder". Making nice with the addiction, disease or illness isn't the way to get it out of your life. It's not your friend and it's not real either. It's just a behavior that takes up a lot of your time.

It is the same with any disease, when we talk about it in terms of *My*, we begin to personalize it as the psyche is hearing this. Depersonalize any talk about this disorder. The idea that you didn't ask for "my eating disorder" is also "victim producing". Own that this is a direct result of both learning and entraining your beliefs and behaviors in this and it will help you both distance and reject this behavior.

When we use language to distance ourselves from the behavior it's much more supportive in your recovery. This is not denial; it's clearly claiming your power over this addiction. *I am not an eating disorder, I'm not a number on a scale, I am a human being.*

Add in: probiotics/acidophilus, and steam all veggies; at this point as it's easier to digest in the healing gut helping to reduce gas and bloating. You might think the big raw salad is a great weight loss option; however, it's going to give you a lot of gas and bloating. Probably better to have steamed spinach and kale, carrots etc., and allow the tummy to avoid these kinds of raw vegetables for a while.

For constipation: add in magnesium before bed, and increase water, really it's pretty simple, and this will correct around in about a week. Even my most challenged clients with severe constipation and real panic about not eliminating enough confirmed this worked in completely recovering bowel function. You can also take an Epsom salts bath at night and absorb the magnesium directly through your skin.

"Ricocheting between constipation and diarrhea is correcting now, the other big one is to stay away from hot chili pepper, spicy foods, and curry, for a while. I have been through about 3 months of really challenging bowel issues, until I figured out it was the use of hot spices. It took about 3 months for my bowel to calm down after discontinuing bulimia. And I had to go to pretty bland foods for that time. It healed. And now I can have a little of this and it doesn't upset my bowel at all."

The nausea and discomfort will heal with time as well.

Shopping from a list - taking control of what you buy and what goes into your kitchen

Changes to the way we do things, will change the impulse purchases, and the way we've always done it: "I want to be free to shop, I don't want restrictions", turns out to be a rule that is actually very harmful to your recovery.

Shopping with a list ensures you get what you need, and are not enticed into purchases the stores want you to make. This way you have *control*. Put this one firmly into your challenge: shopping lists.

This challenge is to only shop from a list.

Start with an inventory of food you do want to eat... make a list.

OBJECTIONS:

When I go shopping *Rule*:

"I like to go crazy, buy everything I see, I don't want any restrictions when I shop"

This simple shift can change impulse purchases and help maintain order when we shop for food. This is due diligence, attention to details and really slowing the process down to better serve yourself. You may think "I want to be free to shop. I don't want restrictions", which often leads to purchasing all kinds of "impulse foods". This is "Chop wood, Carry water". *The means, by which we do things, tends to the outcome we secure for ourselves.*

One of my clients took this rule to heart only using her list. However, she saw blueberries covered in dark chocolate, they were the ones in the super big bag and very reasonably priced. In the moment, the list was forgotten; the chocolate covered berries went home and very shortly thereafter a binge. She said, "I just got so excited about the blueberries because they are so good for you and in dark chocolate too."

Shopping with a list ensures you get what you need, and are not enticed into purchases the stores want you to make. This way you have *control,* put this one into action today.

This challenge is to only shop from a list

"Where is the spontaneity in a shopping list? That seems boring."

These old strategies simply have to shift when we have been suffering at the hands of a food addiction. They just have to and telling yourself otherwise is a sure way to keep the old, out of control patterns in place. Where we eat, when we eat, what we eat, and what we buy may generate some anxiety: "I think about food all the time already, now I have to think about it even more to make a list".

If there's impatience and frustration, it will begin to pass as you experience a difference in the amount of control you have around what foods you are buying and bringing home.

Most people with an eating disorder become panicky when they are going to purchase food items. The shopping list keeps it all "normal" and firmly in your control. You only shop from the list. It's that simple.

This is how it works

1: The idea of a shopping list is multi-faceted

We only get what is on the list; it has what *we really need*. It can eliminate the "spontaneous shopping". When we are hungry, or standing in lines waiting to check out faced with all the sugar, candy and chocolate, this ensures we only get what is on the list.

2: For our purposes:

We make a commitment to only shop from the list. If we go into the store and there is something we really needed, **flip the shopping list over, and put that item on the back of the list or start a new list in your phone**. That's right; you are not purchasing this item this trip. This item starts the new list. You can put your shopping list into your phone as an option if you like.

3: Only buy the amount you need

A suggestion for the big box stores, save all the shopping here for the items that are *non-food items*. If you are purchasing food items here, definitely use the list. Super-size "me" in these stores creates a huge shopping bill, and a lot of food, especially if you live by yourself.

4: This takes food shopping out of the crazy zone and keeps shopping for fuel the same as filling your gas tank. You wouldn't overfill your gas tank would you? What would be the point? It respects food as fuel, and takes the treat/celebration/excitement out of food. Food is just fuel.

5: Let's update: "treats" or treat – A positive Re-frame on the concept of a treat

Treats are generally not fuel. They are something sugary, sweet or high in carbohydrates. We don't need these kinds of treats. They are not helpful at all. They don't treat us nicely either, they are full of junk sugars, fructose, sucrose, dextrose, and corn syrup, which are highly addictive and create toxicity in the brain. They are not good food choices for anyone.

What if your concepts around *Treats* changed to making them material items instead of food items?

A new scarf, book or handbag
A sweater or shirt you wanted
A manicure or massage

Treats don't have to equal food. *Food is just fuel.* This concept of "treats" comes out of our childhood when parents bought us something sweet or a treat at Halloween. Then there is Christmas and Easter.

Consider re-framing this word in your mind and equating it with fresh flowers, or a new pillow, a throw for your sofa there are so many "treats" of this type that will last a long time and continue to remind you of just how much you love yourself.

You can also re-frame "treats" to healthy food items acknowledging the great changes you are making in your life right now. What are some healthy food choices that you really enjoy that would be a real treat for you? Make a list, so when you want to treat yourself, choose from this list instead.

6: The new order of food buying

> Be sure you have eaten a solid protein meal before you enter any store for food
>
> Be sure you have eaten before you go into any store (even nonfood stores offer sugary items)
>
> Be sure you are comfortably satisfied
>
> Be sure you have your list, or don't go in there

Food is fuel, treating yourself well and following your wellness plan, of three small meals a day, proteins first and three small snacks is the greatest gift you can give yourself.

7: Have a friend or relative that offers treats? "Let's go for an ice cream or a soda?"

They could use a little assistance, share what you are doing. When you feel the "resistance" to doing what you know works, just stop and have a chat with yourself. Remind yourself this is the new way and that was the old way. Check, when was the last time you ate?

> We shop from a list
> We don't go shopping when we're hungry
> Food is just fuel, it's not a *treat*
> Check what the voice in your head is saying

"I can't do this, I don't have to be this rigid, I don't need another mother telling me what to do, I know what I'm doing, and I feel like throwing in the towel, this is boring."

Pay attention here, that's the addictive voice. Really? My addiction has a voice? Yes, hear it identify this voice clearly. When you hear it trying to derail your efforts, change the voice. Change the tone, change the sound, make it the voice of your favorite comedians and laugh right out loud. You might even turn the volume down completely and go enjoy your evening doing something else.

The next time you are in a non-food store, notice when you're waiting in line to checkout, how much chocolate, candy and cookies are strategically placed around you at eye level. These stores know what they are doing, it's marketing. The checkouts till in most stores are surrounded with these kinds of sweet sugar laden foods, at marked down prices to entice you to buy.

After shopping, we're tired, and sugar seems like a pick me up. Stores know our weakness; this is another reason to **eat**

before you go shopping, so you are *not tired or experiencing a low blood sugar moment.* **Remember they are not on your shopping list.**

If you have a list that you follow then these places won't mess with your program, or your life, or your weight. Notice "Listen" has the word list in it "Listen to the list, instead of the inner voices."

Sounds like a plan....

8: Always eat before you shop. I don't have to say much about this, however, if you make this a rule of thumb for yourself, you will never again go crazy in a store. When your body is satisfied, it can carry out detailed and complex processes without losing focus and abandoning the activity.

This is critical to your success; eat before you shop for food.

Strategies for Shopping

- Shop only from a list you create at home during the week
- Make the list at home, or your cell phone, keep your list with you
- Only purchase items from the list
- If you see something else, start another list
- Keep the list on hand
- If you forget the list and can't remember it all, go back and get it

- If you think, "I just need this or that", then you are starting to cheat on your list
- Your list is your salvation and your guide
- For the next 90 days shop with a list
- Always eat before you go into a store to get your food items
- Notice how you have less anxiety around shopping for food

Shopping from a list catches all these impulse buys and protects you from these kinds of purchases.

EXERCISE FOR THIS CHALLENGE:

Begin each day with rising at the same time. Endeavor not to stay in bed, get up and get going. These old self-indulgent behaviors are not the best for your recovery now. Let your body know you mean business. Let's go.

Eat your first small protein rich meal within 30 minutes of rising. This sets the optimum rate for using calories consumed in the day and morning snack follows about 2-3 hours later.

A small lunch, selected from vegetables, proteins and fruits (steamed, warmed where possible).

Snack again between 3-4 pm (one of the most important times of day and most of us miss this one waiting for dinner, you may find you are starving and frantic around food. This is just low blood sugar and it's totally OK to eat your protein snack late, and still eat dinner).

Dinner between 5-7 pm choose your time, and endeavor to be complete by 7 pm.

Now put your runners on and head out for a 20 minute walk, if you have children or a dog, it's great for spending time with them. The rest of the evening is relaxed and calm and if you can find your way to bed a few hours before midnight, the restorative sleep is even better.

SLEEP AIDS: Dandelion supplements or tea really help with deeper sleep. Dandelion is an herb that works brilliantly on calming the liver. It's the liver that keeps us up all night, processing – processing. Active scary dreams are often an active liver. Dandelion is a great way to ensure a quiet liver and a deep and delicious sleep.

Add Magnesium into your night-time routine, as this will help with your bowel movements and a deeper sleep as well, use acidophilus if you find your tummy upset or bloated before bed, and you will awake with a relaxed tummy in the morning.

Supplements: Evening primrose, vitamin E, vitamin B100 complex, assists with healing the soft tissue and absorption, B12 is essential improving absorption through the bowel.

Avoid sugary foods at night. These types of foods will keep us up. Often a desire for food at 10 pm is really a signal it's time for bed. Avoid caffeine's and even de-café coffee and tea after 4 pm in the afternoon as this can interrupt sleep.

Exercise for this Challenge:

CHASING HUNGER:
MY WELLNESS PATH

A goal without action will never be met; action without a goal will get you nowhere; a goal with action is achieved without much effort at all. - **A. Beck**

This is the key to your new wellness plan, unique to you - and it's yours to create now

Take your time to go through these set of questions that will help you design your own very powerful wellness plan. Endeavor to keep your comments to "feelings". It's really helpful as its then from the body and how you feel about this. If you feel a little overwhelmed or challenged time to use your "reframing" skills. Take some breaks and come back to it. This is just the start of the changes you want to secure for yourself.

We know there's a benefit behind every behavior or we simply would not do it. Ensure you have recognized where there might be hidden agendas or secondary gains to old behaviors. This is often where self-sabotaging will up-end your best intentions.

Be sure all your goals consider the needed resources you will use.

First: Identify what you want:

What are my beliefs about this behavior?

Am I really clear now about how much damage I've been doing to my health? Am I in denial?

What do I gain from continuing in this pattern? Is there a double bind I've caught myself in?

Am I willing to re-frame what I tell myself about bulimia in order to get well?

Have I recovered my childhood and its effects on my beliefs about healing?

How do I sabotage my recovery?

To turn all this around, what are the steps I'm now willing to take to support my health and well-being?

What would a wellness path look like to me? Do I know the steps needed to achieve this?

Do I feel worthy of this relationship with myself and ready to heal my body and mind?

Spirituality

I don't have to be religious to have a spiritual life, am I willing to bring meditation and relaxation techniques into my life now? If so, can I set a time that works daily?

Would changing my spiritual beliefs now increase my ability to have greater access to recovery?

Does my family have a different view about this? How do they relax? What if I shared I was doing this with them? Do I stop my own growth because of what others will think of me?

How would these spiritual opportunities increase my access to the relaxation response?

I know meditation can reduce my anxiety; however am I skeptical about giving this a fair shot?

Have I given meditation a fair shot in my life, or do I continue to complain about wanting to, but never commit to doing a meditation test?

Spontaneity and Creative expression

What do I get really excited about doing?

Do I know what my passion is in this lifetime?

If you aren't sure right now, think back to when you were 7 years old, what did you want to be?

What helps me to free up my creativity?

Do I do this regularly?

What did I love to do as a kid?

What would I create if I had all the funds available?

Am I willing to express myself creatively?

What does my family believe about my creativity and creative projects?

Sexuality/Sensuality

Am I interested in sex? Have I lost my "libido"?

Have I hidden my sensuality from others and myself?

Do I honor this part of my body and my life?

Am I ashamed of my sexuality? How often do I give or receive touch?

Do I put it off with denying how important it is in my life?

Is there still healing needed around my sexual experiences from the past?

What turns me on, what doesn't? Do I have shame about my body?

Do I feel sensual when I'm not having sex?

What does my family belief about sex?

Relationships:

Do I need to make changes within relationships that I have now?

What about my family? Am I ready to own my behavior and the damage it's done to these relationships? What do I need to change? Make a list in your journal.

Can I forgive these others? Can I forgive myself?

What are the relationship patterns that keep repeating in my life?

How vulnerable am I willing to be in my life and with whom?

What do I derive from the belief: I can save, rescue or change others?

Who am I the go-between for and have my efforts been very effective?

What do I get out of doing this? What belief does it feed in my life? Do I often end up with no thanks for my efforts and people angry with me?

Who would be most upset if I fully recovered and was no longer feeling guilty, shameful or needy?

What would happen to my sense of self if I left others to figure out their own problems and didn't offer to rescue, coach or save them?

Am I aware of just how much I judge others?

Do I judge other women, their bodies, and their behavior?
Do I judge that man for being with that woman? Do
I judge my parents behavior and relationships? Do I
endeavor to rescue adults in my life?

Do I feel worthy of love and compassion and would I be
prepared to give this to myself now?

What is my purpose for this life?

What did I most want to be when I was seven years old? (if
you can't remember your mother or grandmother might
be able to help you – ask them)

Is what I'm doing now even close to that desire I had as a
child?

If not how difficult would it be to begin to take steps to
getting closer to that desire?

What do I think about what I'm doing now? Does it have
value and purpose?

Am I making a difference in the world?

If my financial needs were met would I do something
different?

Is my job a good teacher? Do I learn daily? Do I feel growth
is a big part of my work?

Money:

Does having money generate anxiety?

Have I come to a place where I can't trust myself with
money?

What do I need to do to take care of this?

Does my family have issues with money?

Do I believe money is the root of all evil or creates problems and causes divorces?

If I changed my beliefs around money and finances would anyone be upset with me?

Do I find stressing about money is part of my daily thought process?

My daily life

Do I like to be in nature? How often do I give myself this time?

Am I hoarder? Would I be embarrassed to have someone come to my house right now?

How can I eliminate unnecessary clutter from my life?

Do I walk past piles of stuff I have not touched for weeks, and ignore it all using bulimia instead?

How often to I bathe, wash my hair, and brush my teeth? Are these self-care habits something I do daily, or do I at times neglect basic self-care?

Happiness and joy

What makes me happy?

Are past errors and traumas still my go to excuse for behaving this way?

Do I still coach myself with "that happened, I deserve this"

How much time do I spend complaining, gossiping about others, judging others?

How much time does my inner self, spend negatively judging me?

Exercise and physical recovery

Eating balanced meals, letting food become fuel, practicing the 80/20 rule, correct portion sizes.

This is going to take care of the binge eating and allow the body and brain to recover.

Will I follow the directions I've been given to make this happen? Or will I deviate and blame others?
Will I commit, or will I sabotage?
Will I allow myself to sleep instead of staying up and eating?
Is health and wellness important to me?
What happens if I'm optimally healthy?
What would others say about that?

Acceptance and Commitment:

How much do I love and accept myself with all my divine imperfections, right now?
How much permission do I give myself to make mistakes?
Am I willing to fiercely love, protect and accept myself during this next 90 days?
Do I feel I have everything my body and mind needs to achieve this right now?

Have I now:

Examined and accepted the places where I was sabotaging my recovery?

Investigated beliefs and re-framed them, knowing beliefs are not real, they are just beliefs.

Who is going to help me achieve and maintain my wellness path the best?

List 1 or 2 people that are close to you and support your recovery that you can count on

Have I identified those close to me that trigger or sabotage my wellness path, and if so what have I done about those relationships?

List your doctor and therapist – are they on board with your wellness path now?

Have I fully examined the underlying issues and know the steps I need to take to secure the outcome for the next 90 days?

This is the framework for your wellness path and when all areas are in alignment you will be in the process of recovery. The 90 day challenge will propel you into action.

Some last quick checks:

It's critical to fiercely examine your inner tenacity now: Are you living in isolation and loneliness? Is this self-imposed using Bulimia as the behavior to fill time? What are you going to do with your new found free time? Is someone taking up all your time and space and you don't know how to tell them without losing the relationship? Is your job stressing you out far too much?

Are there any current behaviors you do that create obligation or resentment? Are there people you must check in with each week, calls you must make, and others that make you feel obligated through guilt?

Can you step back from all of this for the next 90 days?

You are now committed to taking full responsibility for your health and wellness plan. You know, no one else can do this for you, you wouldn't let them anyway. You are the determining factor in your recovery now and it's really always been up to you. Feel that power right now, take a deep breath in and mix it inside with your other positive anchored states.

Tackling these bigger questions can seem overwhelming; however, if you have identified the areas of concern, you will be aware of them and not allow them to undermine your recovery. Remember *once you know, you cannot un-know* and once you have identified those root issues you can take steps, even small ones to limit the affects those situations have on your life.

You are the one in charge; you know you always have been. It's your choice, it's your time, you have decided. *Enough is enough, I'm done with bulimia. It just never made any sense anyway. Bulimia was just a waste of my time, and I'm done with it now, and forever.*

Right now you know every step you take towards healing is a step in the right direction. It's not going to be easy, however, if you follow these steps give it your best effort, you like many others, will achieve a successful outcome. You will do it. Days will turn into weeks, and weeks into months, before you know it, you have stopped using food in this way and recovered your life.

You won't believe how good you feel:

"Just wanted to say I have been in the best mood these past few days and I'm not really sure why. I have been eating healthy and not tempted to those old behaviors. I have been social and productive and happy. I just feel like a different person. I am really trying to remind myself that old behavior wastes so much time. Precious time I don't have to spare. I'm not fully happy with my weight but I am reminding myself that it's not the defining aspect of me as a person. It's nice to be in this mindset."

The isolation served the bulimic behavior however, without bulimia in your life, it's time to begin to reach out to others and invite communication and openness. What if I get hurt? Well, it could happen; however, if you have done the work in this book, you will have many new skills to help you feel better about yourself. Maybe allowing yourself to feel your feelings fully now, is really going to help you re-frame that old belief that it's better to avoid pain. Pain is a part of life, part of growing up. It's part of living. Isolation and loneliness really harm your beliefs about life. Now you know how to re-frame those old beliefs. You are doing it!

"Things have never been better. It's been two weeks since I have last engaged in the eating disorder and I feel like a completely different person. I am even letting myself go out on dates with someone I recently started seeing. It's crazy. I don't have any urges to engage or anything and I am really not sure why. I love it!"

You are ready to do this, ready to claim your recovery. Every step towards wellness is a step in the right direction. In this you cannot fail:

You have your list of criteria from each of the 9 challenges

You have your MP3's downloads

You have your book and cards to support you and you have let go of doing it *perfectly*

Close your eyes and let your mind drift into a quiet place

If the inner dialogues start up, take a deep breath in, follow your breath and thoughts will quiet

Open your eyes and review the items on your new wellness path

Listen deeply to the inner wise self; it's right there supporting you, from within. Listen to the guidance being offered to you now and slowly as you read each step, write down the thoughts from that deep inner loving and wise self

Write it down – you don't have to do anything right away – just journaling your insights from the deepest part of you

If you hear something that seems preposterous, like "maybe it's time to find a new job", just write it down

The inner wise self is so loving and so caring it does not offer negative harsh suggestions it will only offer you positive suggestions and generally things you can achieve, trust it

This opens the greatest communication to your inner wise self and the more you listen to it, the more it will be there to assist you in every situation

These 90 days will facilitate a real change and there is no "perfect" needed

Just one step at a time, and before you know it, the days and months are passing and you have reclaimed your life from bulimia

Draw that line in the sand, *I'm done with bulimia and I'm ready to face my life*

The excited anxious feelings are really all just the signal that you are ready to do this

I know it's challenging, this is a big life change, but you can do it

As you move forward, become your own best friend, and trust your inner wise self

If you can't take action right now, and you just don't trust the wellness path fully, know that you might need more help and I'm here. If you choose to wait, that's OK too, however, going forward you will have this information and you can try small things to help you.

Let go of the outcome, it won't be perfect, it's not supposed to and believing it should be is just the ego endeavoring to protect you. Recognize it and let it be an opportunity for great compassion for yourself

There will be ups and downs, slips and falls, however, when you let go of the outcome, you can apply that 80% of the time *I'm following as closing as I can do right now*

You have already given yourself a great shift from what your life was before. Begin to look at all the places you have achieved greater healing and just keep on keeping on

Many people when they start along the path to recovery feel they need to do it perfectly and really you can only do the best you can in the moment. Let go of your despair when things seem they are not going as well as you judge they should and just go back to following what you know works

The wellness plan for me:

What will this look like?
What will it feel like?
What are some of the sounds you might hear associated with achieving this outcome?

Does your outcome involve anyone else?
Can you maintain the process now to reach your outcome?

Secondary gains and self-sabotage:

A secondary gain for our purposes is where some seemingly negative or problematic behavior actually carries out some positive function for us on another level. A secondary gain of bulimia is a belief that it will control my weight. We know it is not an effective weight loss solution as it seriously compromises the body's systems.

What do I need to achieve this goal of being bulimia free in 90 days?

Make your list. Have you ever done this before?

Do you know anyone who has achieved this or a similar result?

Have you achieved other goals? (Quit smoking, quit drinking alcohol?)

What did you tell yourself then? What images did you see in your mind? What feelings?

Was it what you smelled, and that repulsed you? Use the smell of vomit to make bulimia disgusting

What strengths do you have that would be useful to help you achieve this goal?

Have you written them down? Are they easily accessible?

If you don't recover this time what will happen?

If you do recover are there any areas that might be compromised?

Have you covered those off in your wellness check list?

Use a shopping list – avoid buying wrong goods

Eat small portions, six times a day – avoids weight gains

Will actually lose bloating and water retained weight – benefit

Will lose the puffy face and dark circles - benefit

Is this the right time for me:

Can I achieve the desired outcome with the current inner states that I have now?

- To change the inner states I need to follow the exercises in the book
- I need to download the MP3's
- I need to create the right list for me that will keep me on task
- Follow the directions daily until the new path becomes my wellness path
- Can I see myself in 90 days free of bulimia?
- Do I have the sounds, images, words and feelings of the desired outcome firmly in my mind?

Steve Andreas (NLP Trainer and author) shared a great way to shift up a common inner dialogue and let the brain register a new understanding of that phrase *"I can't do it"*.

I CAN
not
DO IT

Notice how it changes the inner strategy to one of **I CAN, DO IT**

Love for yourself as self- compassion opens your heart; gratitude and thankfulness every day will keep you humble, positive and flowing.

CHALLENGE 7:

MINDFUL CONNECTION

Thoughts, we all have them, only some people know it's just a thought. Others terrified of the thought feel compelled to take action. Recognizing the inner thoughts are just thoughts, these are not set in stone, *I have to* thoughts are just thoughts. They don't mean anything, and you can change your thoughts easily. Here we learn the positive application of the well placed "re-frame".

MY PERSONAL STRATEGIES FOR RECOVERY:
WHAT WORKS FOR ME

WHAT IS A STRATEGY?

Literally it's how you do something. When you decide to take a shower in the morning, you make some images, check with your feelings (Yes, I'm going to do this) check the ecology of it (now or later, do I have the soap, shampoo, did someone else use all the hot water) then get a final yes feeling and make your decision. Shower now? Shower later? And then go for it.

We all have strategies like this for everything we do. We are always thinking about things, making images of what it will look like, sound like, feel like, smell like, taste like.

Let's look at the strategies and beliefs supporting avoidance:

A client shared she had an encounter with a care provider that seemed judgmental about her recent increase in muscle. She felt violated and angry. Leaving the therapists office without saying anything she was in a very vulnerable state. It was so triggering around all the times and places where she felt judged about her body. It triggered all the negative internal beliefs and dialogue from all the years of using bulimia and left her feeling angry, violated and exhausted.

Bulimia is a secret disorder, one that is hidden from the closest people around you. Often it's the safe guarding of the secret that keeps our walls up and closed tightly around us. It takes a lot of courage to be seen by others or even one other, to share deep intimacies, *"In-to-me-see"*. We fear our warts, our baggage, our hurts and our beliefs about what has happened to us. We can feel very vulnerable and naked. We can feel so judged.

Sending back a note to this client about her experience helped her re-frame and heal this upsetting experience:

Right now, I feel a lot of gratitude for your friend; she helped all this come forth and facilitate deeper healing. It's not what she thinks, it's what you think that is important, and she very beautifully released your inner judge so you could see it clearly. I hope you have gained a little muscle that means your body is no longer consuming the muscle; it's using fat for fuel. I'm glad to hear she noticed more muscle. Your body is recovering.

Let's look at some artful "reframing" of this experience:

Imagine saying this to yourself now:

"I'm pretty sure what she said was meant as encouragement; to know you are going in the right direction. However, that she spoke at all about my body has triggered the old stuff really so I can clear it."

__A recovery ceremony__: print this out, take it and burn it. As you watch the smoke go up and out, promise yourself you will not get into these thoughts against yourself again. Hear her voice and how she meant it, "you are doing great, here's the affirmation, muscle. You are awesome." And none of these feelings or thoughts, or what she said or didn't say, equals bulimia.

Sometimes when we speak our truth we begin to get advice in return, this is not honoring heartfelt intimacy either. When our boundaries have not been respected in the past, we know this takes time for us to begin to experiment and test the relationships when sharing with others.

Trust and intimacy takes time. Test the waters, feel it out. If trust is broken, bring this to their attention, and if they will not respect it, just step back a little. You don't have to make it punitive, or create a lot of tension or drama. Raging against the injustices of others is the old way. It's time to step forward and speak your truth.

What is being vulnerable?

When you identify and claim your feelings: If you're fearful, own it. If you don't have the immediate answers say you don't know. If you made a mistake, just say you did it. When you own your feelings you can take appropriate action. Embrace the notion that we might fail or get hurt. It happens.

Take the risk, reach out, and ask for assistance. When you acknowledge you need help it gives you the chance to be receptive and you make room for other people to participate in your life too.

In what area of your life are you afraid of being rejected? Can you tolerate the possibility of being rejected? Through action comes growth. Risk it, you are worth it. Take a bold step and see how it feels, how it works out, and what you learn from chancing rejection. It's a risk, can you survive feeling rejected?

Numbing our negative feelings, we also numb our positive ones too. Feelings are feelings the depths of our sorrows enables us to fully feel the real wonders of our highs. It's all connected. Feeling vulnerable is to be alive — to exist as your most beautiful authentic self and is the challenge of your lifetime.

Setting appropriate boundaries – a lesson in vulnerability

When you take powerful steps to help yourself become more authentic and begin risking your inner world there is value in taking "baby steps". When you share with someone that seems critical or judges you, it's OK to share how you feel. You can tell them about it. This is a big risk, what if they get angry or refuse to accept what you are telling them?

This might feel like it's so overwhelming. Many times in the past, these feelings of avoiding painful interactions ended in using bulimia to blank out hurt and disappointment, now we're suggesting something different.

How to confront someone's behavior, so you are heard, they don't attack you or feel attacked by you

Generally when you use "I" statements people don't get defensive. Generally they will listen and endeavor to understand how you feel about what has happened. They have a choice as to how to proceed from there and so do you. Most importantly you have spoken your truth.

A suggested response she could consider:

"Recently I've been doing recovery work on my use of an eating disorder. When you mentioned my "weight gain" and noticing muscle, I felt judged and shocked that you would say anything to me about my body, especially with regards to gaining weight. For a moment it brought up all the old feelings of panic and anxiety. I want you to know how I felt and that it was not OK with me".

Done, you don't have to argue, support your comments or anything else. You have said your piece.

There is nothing harmful in expressing yourself in this way. What other people do with your expression around your personal boundaries is up to them as well. The therapist might feel stressed that she upset you, and you can accept her conscious apology with grace. You spoke your truth.

Let's look at this experience for what it is: first it's an acknowledgment of what happened and that you spoke up on your own behalf. You are not denying your feelings, or ignoring them. It does not criticize them for their lack of sensitivity, it just says this is how it went for me and it was upsetting. "I" statements are a very clean and sincere expression of feelings. They also show respect for yourself and the other person, because you put voice to your feelings demonstrating you value them and the relationship enough to speak up, not just find a different massage therapist.

Boundaries that are respected keep everyone safe; having good boundaries precludes the need for control because those boundaries work for everyone. When boundaries are not respected this generates feelings of insecurity, a lack of safety and the need for excessive control.

It's recommended you deal with your hurt feelings before you take any steps towards expressing what you felt. Feel the hurt burning away as you watch the flames consume the page taking with it, all the emotions, the feelings, the hurt and suffering. This helps you bring back into perspective the comments from this person and realize they weren't meant to inflict pain. She simply touched a deep wound you had been carrying for a long time.

In the past you demonstrated a lack of honoring boundaries around yourself and others, which created issues of distrust especially with yourself. This is a decision to reset these boundaries. If you honor them, respect them, respect other's boundaries you will find you begin to value yourself and feel a new level of confidence in expressing what you want.

State what is important to you, and then move forward. If the situation continues, this might be a relationship you need to set new limits and boundaries with.

"Thank you for your note, I am still crying now because I feel so heard, understood. Thank you for your encouragement Kathy. This is very helpful. I will work on the reframing and follow with the ceremony. I appreciate you speaking to my soul's soul.

Strategies are how we make our way through life's events. There is a strategy for anger, for joy, for frustration and even love. If we buried all these emotions using bulimia it can seem really scary starting to let ourselves experience them again.

The complex equivalence re-frames: The strategy of bulimia

The need for excitement is an old anchor from our childhood. What can I do with my feelings of boredom? I'm bored equals I need to do something, there's nothing to do. I'm going to reward myself with food and binging and purging. The complex equivalency of Bulimia and Eating Disorders:

- I'm bored = Plan for bulimia
- I need excitement = what can I eat?
- I'm angry, they should not have said that = I'm going to binge and purge
- She noticed my body changes = She must be judging I'm getting fat; I have to binge and purge
- My mother checks on what I've eaten = She doesn't trust me to know what's right for me
- My boyfriend contacted a therapist for help with ED = He has to go, he doesn't get this
- My thoughts make me want to binge on food = Start the planning
- I'm late for work = I'll call in sick and indulge my self-pleasuring today
- Planning for the weekend, everyone's away = Binge and purge weekend

Shifting these strategies is much easier than you think. It starts with maintaining the food as fuel support for your body. If these kinds of edgy internal dialogues start up, it's time to interrupt the patterned thinking and do something different and *right now.*

EXERCISE FOR THIS CHALLENGE:

When the "I'm bored" feeling begins, recognize it's the strategy to fire off this pattern of behavior. What do you feel first? Where is the feeling in the body? Slow everything down, take it step by step and begin to break apart the things you are saying to yourself and the feelings you are having. Describe them here:

Is there a sense of urgency, frantic eating and rushing the binge?

Slow this down. Move to a second or third perceptual position and observe yourself

Write out your experiences here: Does it slow down the process?

Where do you feel the feelings?

What happens next?

Can you think clearer in the different perceptual positions?

Does it give you more control?

Imagine stepping back from the scene, can you gain more control here?

What do you tell yourself?

Have you been restricting food a little?

What do you see?

How clear is it, can you change the images, take the colour out, shrink it down?

What are you hearing yourself say to yourself?

What tone are you using?

Is it your voice or someone else's? Could you change the voice?

Where is the voice coming from?

What do you feel in your body?

Does the feeling change? Or move? From where to where?

In your own mind, see yourself just stepping out of your body and taking two steps back:

Now what do you observe?

What happens if you were to slow everything down?

Change the voice, make it someone's voice that makes you laugh

What happens to the urgency?

Where are the feelings in your body now?

Know thy triggers – avoidance, I don't want to have to deal with how I feel

The various rules and assortment of beliefs you live your life behind distracts and avoids. Avoiding has been one of the permission triggers to use bulimia. The days, one after another of swearing, this is over, I will change this tomorrow, I will stop and I will never do this again. Take a few moments now, and respond to this exercise fully. Once you know yourself, you can't pretend you don't know.

Pain avoiding has driven the behaviors associated with bulimia as much as any other belief. Using bulimia has helped distract the feelings allowing the behaviors to take over and dispel the emotions.

Anger has real fire in it, and it can feel overwhelming. If anger wasn't safe to express we often cover it by avoiding interactions of this type and simply bury the feelings with the addictive behavior.

Recognize feelings and emotions are there for purpose they help us find our deepest wounds so we can do something about them. The therapist didn't mean to cause you pain or trigger your past with her comments; however, because she did, it lets you know you have found the deep wound and it's time to heal.

Start by forgiving the innocent comments and the person that delivered them. Can you give yourself as much forgiveness as you forgive another?

Secondary Addictions are lethal – when we are dealing with one addictive and compulsive behavior and add in a secondary one sometimes thinking "this helps the first one", you are literally mixing brews. It will not end well and often makes the primary addiction even stronger.

Alcohol & recreational drugs complicate bulimia. When you use them you have two problems the addiction to bulimia and now you are adding more addictive substances. Alcohol turns to sugar; direct into the blood stream and used in excess will create another addiction for you. Alcohol works with the same pleasure centers in the brain as bulimia. Alcohol is simply adding in empty calories.

Alcohol and recreational drugs are not options for you during the next 90 days. Their use will undermine your determination and strip you of the necessary resolve. You need all your resources to support your desire to break free for the last time.

If you find this a bit challenging these suggestions might be helpful:

Switch to sparkling water for beverage choices
People today are endeavoring to drink less alcohol, soft
    drinks and sugary beverages; it will be an easy substitute

for you; water, herbal tea or sparkling water are all great
    choices, have them ready and available on hand at home
Remove all alcohol from your home and don't buy any more
Remove all old alcohol bottles and stashes you have at home,
    give it away if you must
Drinking buddies, get them on side with you or park those
    relationships at the curb for the next 90 days

All we have to do with our friends that use drugs and alcohol
is let them know we're not going to indulge for the next 3
months and they disappear anyway. Test it out it might
surprise you how fast they disappear and become busy
elsewhere.

Use your unique talent and ability to become absolutely
driven and determined to do something and apply it to this
90 day challenge. I will do this; *nothing is going to stop me.*

Some people envy others with the kind of logical
determination you have. If you smoked, they envy that you
stopped smoking and it didn't bother you a bit. Remember
that feeling when you realized smoking was simply a waste
of time, unhealthy, smelled terrible and used up a lot of
money? People recognize smoking as addictive behavior; a
smoker is someone who is controlled by a substance. You
stopped and showed them, *nothing controls me.*

Well bulimia has been controlling you, and you have
been letting it. Are you tired of being controlled yet? Feel
that personal power now, feel how much you enjoy others
envying your ability to just stop an addictive behavior,

just like that. You know when you want to do something, *nothing stops you.*

Enough is enough, I'm done with bulimia. It really makes no sense at all.

The unwavering inner resolve to do this, whether challenged by relationships, emotions, personal fears and frustrations; there remains that inner resolve which is your personal mastery. The will to succeed is there supporting you now. Feel it. Feel that inner resolve and power increasing and anchor this state in you right now, as you breathe deeply feel the feeling increasing and now press your finger and thumb together and add this to your personal *best states.*

The mind is yours to command. Feel your own power, heighten it now and you will achieve this, you can do this. You know you can do anything you put your mind to. Moment to moment you cannot fail because you have the key when you want something, *nothing stops you.*

There is nothing that stops me nothing.

Taking care of what is important to you first

1: Listen to your voice, hear the tone, the inner voice will replicate it with urgency, anxiety or frustration. Hear that voice and just as you might with a child, calm it down. Move the voice to another position, soften it, and take the anxious energy out of it. Slow it down and calm it down, take breaths between the words and experience the release of tension in your body. Hear your own voice with soothing tones encouraging you to stay the course.

2: Day to day, review your schedule and the foods that you have prepared and are eating. Small portions, protein rich, at scheduled times in the day and relax enjoying the foods, knowing that more is coming in the next few hours. This is the key to your success and remaining steadfast with this will ensure you achieve it. Food is just fuel, it's not a game, a reward or something to get excited about; it's just fuel.

3: Pay attention to portion sizes, this is a critical key; eat protein that is the size of the palm of your hand in snacks and meals. Get carbohydrates from fruits and vegetables while keeping the wheat products to the smallest amount of your overall food consumption.

4: Check all the packaged ingredients as you clear out your cupboards and refrigerator to start. Simply dispose of anything that contains fructose, dextrose, corn syrup or sucrose. These sugar derivatives are more addictive than street heroin and are toxic to your system.

5: Exercise about 3-4 times a week, just 20 minutes each time will keep you strong and healthy. Add swimming and yoga for variation, team sports for participation and community.

6: Mindfulness decreases anxiety. In today's world we are bombarded with anxiety from all directions. Anxiety and panic attacks seem to be common experiences of everyday life. You have the keys to change this, by simply using your meditation recordings daily or at a minimum, three times a week. You will find challenging moments are merely moments of reflection and greater awareness.

Mindfulness is a mental state achieved by focusing one's awareness on the present moment, while calmly acknowledging and accepting one's feelings, thoughts and bodily sensations.

Focus on your in drawn breath and now follow the exhale out of your body; the mind is focused on the breath, clear of other thinking. Let's try that again; mindful of breath.

7: Accept yourself, just as you are. You are ever changing. How you treat yourself is reflected in your eyes and your face, the way you hold yourself, your walk, your talk, your every movement, this is important. How you talk to yourself inside is how you treat yourself on the outside. Each morning before you get out of bed, take a moment and say to yourself:

"I accept myself just as I am, right now."

Did you know the voice inside your head is the most important voice you listen to? In fact it's the only voice you ever truly listen to.

8: Bring a new level of awareness to how you speak to yourself. How you take care of your body. You can look great on the outside, but if inside you are hearing critical thoughts about yourself, it encourages a sense of low self-esteem and self-worth.

Daily: Moderate exercise to improve self-love and self-acceptance, as both increase self-esteem.

"I accept myself just as I am, right now".

After the first 30 days of this exercise of self-acceptance, add to it: "I love and accept you just as you are", and another "I love you just as you are" after dressing and getting ready for your day.

After practicing this for 30 days, anyone around you that is critical of you or others your mind will instantly reject the negative commentary. You will notice how it makes you feel. How your mind "depresses" with this kind of behavior. It just doesn't feel good.

Gravitate towards people that are positive about how they feel towards themselves, because it is just so much easier for them to like everyone else too, including you, and you will find you feel the same way about others again.

It's called positive internal self-talk and I recommend it daily

The more you practice this the better you will get at it. I know at first it's going to feel a little strange but do it anyway, that's why I suggest you do this when you first awake. Before you get out of bed, before your head starts to argue with you, and present all the arguments that this just can't be true.

"I love and accept myself, just as I am". This is a complete re-frame on all the other things you have sometimes heard yourself say. After a few days of hearing it, some of those "other things" will drop away – because they aren't true and they never were.

9: Get really fierce with yourself around the concept of *perfection*. Say it every morning, "perfect is not about me". Perfect is for cushions that match the chair but this is not a word to describe you, or how you look. There is no perfect you. Catch yourself when you are saying this to yourself, and opt for better language. Be ready to re-frame 'perfect' *the minute you hear it!*

"I used to tell myself I was" - *Now I tell myself; I accept myself just as I am; I don't define myself in this way.* I used to remind myself often of how hard my mom and I were on each other, now I am the hero in the story about my relationship with my mother."

Be the hero in all your stories about yourself. You don't have to embellish them, however, be in a positive place whenever you talk about yourself. Drop out of those "complaining conversations"; you know the ones where everyone complains about some part of their life, their body or job or relationship? Just stop talking about yourself this way; they don't make anyone feel good. That's right, *stop complaining* and *start appreciating*. Find what is good, and talk about that.

Clearing Limiting Beliefs

Have you ever found yourself saying that you want to do something, and then giving up because it becomes just too overwhelming? Let's just re-frame that right now: If you are honest with yourself, anything you have ever put your mind to, *you have done it.*

We have family members and they remember stories about us as children or when we were growing up. These stories are someone else's story about us, or who they think we are, but now we know, the only voice they are listening to is their own. This is just their "internal dialogue" you are listening to, and it was never about you in the first place. Not until you started to believe it and then tried to make it real.

Sometimes we repeat these stories because we aren't really sure, or have not been thinking that clearly about what we have been doing. The stories become affirmations for continuing. In the beginning you had to tell yourself I want this, and then really work at it. Let's be honest, some days it doesn't work. And some clients are actually bulimic and have gained a lot of weight too.

That old story is not who you are, not at all. Now you know this is just a limiting belief. And those old limiting beliefs present as persuasive "reason" for limiting the options available while keeping you on the same old treadmill.

EXERCISE FOR THIS CHALLENGE:

For each question write out ten points, and then prioritize them, from most important (1) to least important (10) – Ten top points.

- What are your beliefs about bulimia? (10 points)
- What's important to you about bulimia? (10 points)
- Who are you? (Write down ten things about you?
- What's important to you about relationships? (10 points)
- What things could you do to create the desired positive changes right now?
- Name ten thoughts to challenge these old limiting beliefs?
- What beliefs would serve you better now?
- Name 10 new positive affirmations that will keep you on your path?

Bulimia just makes no sense at all, it never really did

Bulimia was only here to save you from a restrictive diet you tried once that didn't have an exit strategy. Bulimia became the exit strategy to interrupt a restrictive diet which had turned into starvation. This 90 day challenge is *now your exit strategy*. Now you know, diets don't work, bulimia has never been about weight loss, and it's an addiction. In fact a proper eating plan such as the one in this book will help your body go to its correct weight, and stay there. You will in fact, become one of the people that never changes your body weight for the whole of your lifetime. You can do this; it certainly can be done, because many have achieved it, I know you can.

CHALLENGE 8:

FORGIVENESS

"The one good thing about the past is it is finally over."

Dr Richard Bandler, co-creator of
Neuro Linguistic Programming
(NLP) and the Society of NLP™

The past is over, it's finally over. It seems obvious but many of us are still stuck in the past reliving and repeating mindless rituals that no longer serve us. Now it's time to set the past free, and let it go. When it's forgiven, it can be released, we've accepted it as is was, we don't continue to compare it to current life issues and it can become "finally and completely over".

Forgiveness is a way of being in the world. It truly denounces "perfection", because no human was ever designed to be perfect we were meant to experience being human. We just decided to make that our focus one day and through brain entrainment, abandoned everything else to the detriment of our physical, emotional and spiritual self, destroying relationships with ourselves and anyone else close to us.

"Forgiveness is not something you do for someone else, and it certainly doesn't make what they did or didn't do for you, right. Nor does it mean you need to spend more time with that person or remain in that relationship the way it was." - **Christiane Northrup, Author of Mother Daughter Wisdom**

Forgiveness is the gift you give to yourself. It's the way to release guilt and shame, it's freeing you from never ending criticism, pain and suffering over a past that no longer exists; forgiveness is the gift that keeps on giving for the rest of your life.

Who do you most need to forgive in your life right now?

Your mother, your father, sisters, brothers, family members

Is there a teacher, or person you held in high regard that let you down?

A friend or special person in your life that really let you down

You?

Make a list here:

_____

_____

_____

_____

_____

Reflections for when you find yourself unwilling to forgive

No one out there is getting treated as badly as you are treating yourself in *here*. *What have they got to complain about? I cancel, refuse to participate, would rather isolate and be by myself rather than with them?*

Family members get the full dose from the "addictive monster within" and they are at a loss as to how to help you, you have not wanted their help, you have wanted your addiction.

Comments like: "I don't want to live this way; no one would". The family feels so badly they leave you alone. Am I up or down? Did I or didn't I? Have I betrayed my body yet again?

When we practice forgiveness, we think it might be easiest to start by forgiving others; however, it's very challenging to really forgive others if you refuse to forgive yourself.

Forgiveness is one of the keys to this challenge and it starts with each new day.

This challenge is to forgive yourself for all that you thought you knew, the belief you should be perfect, the way you behaved towards others, yourself, the waste, and anything else you might want to toss in here. Forgive it all. It doesn't mean it was right it's just time to let it go now, once and for all, and forgive the beliefs and behaviors.

I've too much to forgive; I've hurt so many...

Would you keep a friend that is as un-supportive as you are to yourself?

Do you believe that forgiving requires something from someone else first?

Has this wrong-doing and resentment become part of my identity?

What are the pleasures of this anger and resentment?

Is there a part of me that wants to entertain the anger?

Is it my ego that will not forgive me?

What would forgiveness look like?

Do I want to stay stuck in the drama of this forever?

Do I have a special slant on the story that supports me and not them?

When you notice anger and resentments:

Name the wound
Name the trigger
Name the person
Name the behavior
Where do you feel the feeling in your body?

A little message on forgiveness:

.....The First to apologize is the Bravest
.....The First to forgive is the Strongest
.....The First to Forget is the Happiest

Forgiveness and letting go in your heart:

How do I truly forgive myself and others?

Forgiveness

Forgiveness isn't about turning the other cheek and allowing hurts to continue. You've done this long enough. Forgiveness is about choosing to see through the unconscious actions and figure it out working it through and letting it go for the last time. Some say that shame and guilt held within are the very worst ways to torture ourselves. It's death by a thousand cuts. It's time to let this go once and for all. Enough is enough. You are important, you were meant to be here and you can verify that right now by acknowledging you are indeed here.

As we forgive ourselves it allows us to forgive others and heals the wounds of separation. We are all human; forgiving returns the world to wholeness, returns your world to wholeness and you to your own spiritual divinity.

EXERCISE FOR THIS CHALLENGE

How do you pretend to be perfect? What stories do you tell yourself?
Are they useful, or helpful?
Would you be prepared to forgive yourself for not being perfect?

Healing and forgiveness need only be done once. Like a computer icon on our desktop we can click on the icon and dive directly back into the feelings as often as we want to and it can feel awful. We change icons through forgiving. It's time to start purging these old icons and files now and you are the only one that can do it. That's right we're going to dump them into the waste basket and empty the trash too.

Do I still get that panic, fear or anxiety? We become the icon linking us to those memories, negative stories and feelings. This becomes embedded in the cells of our body and forms the structure of our synaptic connections. We keep checking on that icon, adding life experience after life experience, making it strong and seemingly permanent. But it is not permanent, just like the desktop or screen on your iPhone, it's an icon, a collection of feelings held in a cluster and you can easily drop it in the trash and then, empty the trash too.

What do you need to forgive?

In others:
In yourself:
In your life:
About your body:
And your mind:

Make a list of at least 10 items for each of these categories. Place them on separate pieces of paper. When you are done, roll each one up, and then in a safe place, (sink or fireplace) light each one on fire and watch as it burns away, completely. As you watch, forgive all of it, everything you had on that piece of paper. Forgive it totally and completely. If any gray ash remains, wash it away down the drain.

Now for the big questions of life:

Who am I really?

As we contemplate these bigger questions, we begin to find ways to express our uniqueness and our soul's light in ways that illuminate just who we truly are. Deep inside, somewhere, you know the answer to this question, and it's not a challenge to find it, it's a challenge to listen and accept the love that is there inside you. Your deepest self is so loving and so caring, it will never abandon you, it has not left you, you are not past caring for, it's there, just be still for a minute and listen to that deeper voice. You can always tell the difference between this voice and some of the other things you've sometimes heard yourself say, because this voice, your voice, is so loving, so caring and supportive. Listen, just listen.

Am I important to others?

This question is rich with potential. Think about your parents and your family members, and how much each of them has reached out to help you, with love for you, has worried, stressed, and got angry, said things they wish they hadn't. They've often reacted through fear and hurt. You have done your share too. This is family. Family sometimes interacts in ways that we endeavor to avoid with the rest of the world. It's our primary place of experimenting and developing experience. No one's is perfect, no one. And pretending you can be or will be more perfect than others can mislead your beliefs away from what is real in an attempt to be something other than you are - human.

Perfect is just a word

Perfect is for flowers, or a blue sky day, or even a pillow or a perfect tissue. It's not a concept that was ever intended for humans and yet we apply it to variations of what we consider about ourselves.

Finding ourselves less than perfect we then try to live by those margins. Am I 90% perfect? 75% perfect? Was I, 100% today? Day to day we are changing, moment to moment life is presenting opportunities for us to evolve. Evolution is a staging event; it's ever changing as are we and it was never meant to be "perfect".

When you get stuck on one image, focused on one bad event, fixated, just take a moment and move that still image onto the "next frame" in your inner movie screen. That's right just play it forward until things improved, relaxed and changed. Breathe deeply and let yourself really experience the changed feeling. Notice how the feeling moves differently too.

Ever build a house? Or how about renovate a house or even one room in a house, or how about your own room from time to time? At various stages of the event the project can represent complete chaos and cause ripples of that chaos to affect everything in our lives. Eventually the project comes to an end and seems *perfect* in the final stages. Until you start another one and we're always starting new projects its life. How boring would it be to have only one project in a lifetime, and then that's it: done.

This is evolution at work in our lives and it is the experience we all crave. We are always evolving moment to moment, we are never the same, we can't be and why would we want to be? Your greatest work this lifetime is not "how thin can I be?" It's to discover your passion and purpose for being here. There is only one you, unique and if you don't think you were meant to be here then think of how you got here in the first place. Your 'drive for thinness' is not really a solid weight loss program and it's not your sole purpose in life either. Quite frankly anyone can do what you are doing if they wanted to.

Comparisons to others: masking attention seeking

Attention seeking behaviors are often at the core of this behavior and in can start in our childhood where we often felt we were competing for attention from our parents. Why are they getting more attention than I am? What do I need to do to get that attention focused on me? It might sound self-serving or selfish to want attention focused on you, but isn't that why you want to be so thin? Isn't it about getting everyone to *look at you*? Don't you enjoy the focus, even if it's upset and anxious focus from your parents and others that love you, that intense focus on you, is really all that matters. I want that focus, on me and no one else.

The focus on skinny started as a competition, a diet with no exit strategy, how do I get out of this when my whole focus continues every day: *I must be thinner, I get noticed when I am thinner.* The fatal flaw is the type of attention an addiction gets you isn't really what you wanted in the first place.

Stopping thoughts about weight gain

If you place that focus and attention onto something other than weight the shift is discernible. You can feel the change. You might keep drifting back to fears of weight gain but that is just a thought. Take all the color out of those images, change their sharpness for fuzzy gray ones, and turn down the volume on the sound track. Thoughts are constantly changing, you can't keep the same thought for 1 second, you have to keep reinforcing it or the mind shifts off to another thought. These are your thoughts, you are creating them and you can change them. Cancel them, laugh at them, physically get up and go do something else. After all, you are running your own brain.

A quick note here, if its food you think about all the time, following the eating plan here will get rid of the obsessive thinking about food. Do it for a week, eat six small meals a day, between 7 am and 7pm and then check periodically through the day: am I thinking about food now? Now what will you think about, because you won't gain weight eating this way, in fact your body will take you to your right weight and stay there. No more fluctuations either. No more ups and downs on the scales, just the right weight.

Spontaneous acts of healing: Healing from bulimia for the last time:

We are not supposed to avoid the *negative* thoughts or feelings or emotions we have. These are life *experiences* and they are ours to explore fully. We have feelings to help us make sense of what is happening to us or around us. It's OK to feel these emotions and not judge them as good, bad, or negative, *they are just feelings.* Sometimes we've come to believe that it's not OK to feel our feelings or to express them. Perhaps it made someone else uncomfortable when we were young and we were punished for expressing our feelings. Perhaps others around us were expressing their emotions *loudly* and everyone else had to keep their emotions to themselves. Perhaps it seemed safer to just avoid feelings and emotions altogether. Whatever the reason you can know that feelings: are *all just feelings.*

And we have lots of them every second of every day we are experiencing something. We all have feelings and emotions we don't like or want too. Sometimes we believe we should not be having these feelings. If we were okay in the world we would only have good feelings and emotions. *There must be something wrong with me because I have these other feelings.* The fact is everyone has emotions and everyone has feelings they do not like or want, *and they are still just feelings.*

Healing from the belief we must be perfect and never show anger, upset or negative emotions stops the flow and we begin to live in our own fantasy world. Our parents, our family members, our friends, and teachers all experience feelings. Employers, doctors, lawyers, everyone has emotions and feelings; *everyone, because we are all human.*

And they are just emotions creating a feeling in the body and if you don't like that feeling or the thoughts you are thinking, you can change them. In fact *wait a second* and they will change. How we view something will change it right away. Here you can practice taking all the color out of those images, and changing the internal sound of your voice, to one that is helpful, kind, compassionate, or even funny; make it more powerful or commanding; the sound of your favorite comedian's voice. And just laugh, yes laugh. What makes you laugh right out loud?

How can I stop this kind of thinking?

Rather than replaying the thoughts and images over and over. Bring them to your awareness: I'm feeling really charged right now, I feel really angry about this. I feel really sad or upset, I feel - I feel. Become aware of what you are actually telling yourself. Is it true? Can you actually prove it's absolutely the only truth on that subject right now? Step back and take second position on this, now step back to third position. Do you get a different perspective? Is what you are telling yourself really the only way it is?

If it's not absolutely true and not absolutely concrete and could be different than what you were telling yourself, is there any point to continuing to tell yourself "this is the way it is"?

What if you just stopped, and asked yourself: Is this true?

Challenge those stories you have been told or repeat to yourself daily.

Feel your feelings, listen to your stories.

Step out of the image now, and step to the side so you watch yourself there in the movie and feel you are no longer *in it*. *Maybe you can see this situation was really never about you in the first place.*

Check your feelings now.

- Breathe deeply.
- Check the feelings again.
- Which way are they moving through your body? Could you change that feeling and make it go in the opposite direction? What about making it bigger so it's outside your body? What happens if you breathe deeply and just let go?
- Is your body relaxing?
- Think the same thought, exactly the same as it was when it gave you the feeling.
- Check and feel what you feel now?
- Can you actually laugh a little at what was happening in your mind?
- Check on your feelings now.
- Breathe deeply
- Check again.

Your brain processes the thought without judging it as good or bad and ignores the negative:

Most fears are associated with a version of the future when we look at them in the moment, or focused on a past event that you believe will replicate instantly and give you the direct results. Neither is in the "present moment". That's why they call the "present" the present, because it is a true gift. Here we are free from past and future. The past is over, thank goodness, and the future, it hasn't happened yet!

You are completely free in the moment to do something different.

Remember your brain processes negatives as a positive: **I *don't* want to gain weight = gain weight** because the "don't" doesn't compute. Ever heard that one about **"what you focus on grows"** so focusing on not gaining weight is to focus on "gaining weight".

"What do you mean I can't trust my thoughts?" there it is your unconscious just heard; "trust my thoughts". It doesn't listen to the "can't".

So from this little pattern of words, your deep unconscious just heard: "I want to gain weight and I can trust my thoughts". Let's start over...

Language patterns and how you talk to yourself every moment of the day programs the beliefs that drive your behaviors. These patterns can shift quickly when you bring to consciousness what you tell yourself.

Experience yourself as compassionate, joyful and in the moment. Choose a better thought a better outcome and breathe deeply. Relax. Follow your breath in and out. *And now spin that energy you were feeling in an entirely different direction in your body. Feel the feeling disappear and as it does press the finger and thumb together and breathe deeply. Recall your peaceful calm feelings.*

Nice work! You just changed your feelings and your experience. Spontaneous acts of healing happen when we "get something". It's the Ah Ha moment. *I get it now.* This can release the burden of having to carry that story around with you. That moment of clarity shifts everything. And you just changed it, feel your power shift right now. And you can use this tool any time you want to or need to. It's yours and you earned it. In fact the more you use these tools the better you will become at changing what you feel and the faster it will work for you in the moment when you really need it.

Exercise in how forgiveness heals

When we can't forgive ourselves, we can't forgive others and if we don't love ourselves, we are not much good at loving others either. What does it take to really forgive a person that has been so hard on you, or hurt you, or turned your life upside down when you just wanted to be with them and love them? Forgiving ourselves is sometimes more challenging than forgiving anyone else.

How does projection work?

A simple way to think of projection and projecting on to others is to think of a movie theater, with the projection unit at the back of the theater. We project a construct (something we make up in our own mind) of what we believe is true from our own inner movies recalled through deleting information, adding in things, and generalizing details, projecting it over the other person as "how it must be". It covers the real face of the person we are thinking about or talking to and calling that projection "real" or the "truth". The way it must be, according to our own inner experiences which are very often distortions, generalizations and deleted information; all piles up into one super charged moment.

"There they must be wrong".

It happens when we are not fully aware of our own expectations, desires and judgments; instead we don't take responsibility for our own feelings and try to attribute them to others. A projection can be devilish or divine, disturbing or comforting, but it is a projection just the same. Like a cloud or fog that prevents us from seeing reality as it is. The only way out is to recognize what you are doing, or the other is doing. When you find a judgment arising about another, turn it around: does what you see in another really belong to you? Is your vision clear or clouded by what you want to see?

Projections are really dangerous because people make decisions based on what they have projected onto others and then hold it as true, and it's THEIR truth, not what is real at all. A very dangerous projection is to create that image and hold it as the only truth refusing any other possibility. This is often the projection you have used to create images of yourself which are not necessarily correct.

The neat thing about this is, it's just a projection and because you made it up in the movies of your mind, you can make new ones and delete those old ones just by changing the way you see something, hear the sounds and then access those feelings. "That must be true; I feel it when I think about it" and it's not necessarily so.

The critical awareness is your inner judgments and expectations. Challenge those and you become the master of your inner movies.

EXERCISE FOR THIS CHALLENGE

I want you to know I validate all your pain and suffering and the terrible things that have happened along the path. This is not to minimize or make light of your experience either. It is however, time to let this go. I don't want to leave you caught in those old bitterness's from the past. I can't know all that happened to you, but I do know it's been lonely, sad and isolating; filled with fear and loss. Do this exercise now with a solid choice in your heart to move beyond the past and free yourself from it. Its time, you can do this and I'm right here with you.

Just for a moment, set aside your beliefs about an event or someone you know you want to forgive. It might be a lover, a friend, mom, dad, sibling or another family member. Maybe a favorite Grandparent had to leave you and you felt they stopped loving you and you were hurt and angry.

Close your eyes and imagine or sense that person right now and feel the energy in your body when you think of them. Can you see them fully? Picture them from the top of their head to the bottom of their feet, see their eyes, and notice their appearance, imagine them fully sitting there across from you.

If you can't fully see them, then sense their presence. When it's really filled in for you, check within your own body and see where you most feel the energy in your body from this relationship.

If you could touch that energy what would it feel like? Does it have a color, or a thickness, or prickly feeling? What is it like? Is it hot or cold, soft or strong, metal, or even electric? Now looking at this person, go ahead and tell them out loud, all the things you have wanted to tell them for so long. Feel free to write the words down as you say them, and imagine they are listening to every word. It's really important for you to express your feelings fully. Take your time. Remember all the times and places, and all the things they did or said, and tell them your feelings.

When you are complete with this part, I'd like you to now, check in your own body and feel where you have been sending energy to them. What does it feel like? Can you see or sense the energy? Does it have a texture? Is it dark or light? Where does it leave your body and where does it attach to their body?

Now go ahead and once again, write down any additional things you want them to know. This is your chance, all that stuff you have been saying to yourself for years, things that you told yourself to keep you anchored to this old behavior, get it out there now.

You are safe, this is a very safe way to do this, go ahead. Now I want you to feel those energies and imagine, cutting through them. As soon as you do, those energies go back to that other person and your energy comes back to you. Imagine now, allowing all that energy to float inside your heart, where it turns to pure white energy, creating a heart to heart connection with the person now through this white heart to heart energy, receive the same back from them. Have you any more words to say to them? Speak them out. Write them down.

I want you to know that everything that has been shared here – on a soul to soul level, they got it. They have heard every word and they have listened. Imagine the energy fading now as you let their image fade away. I want you to tell them you forgive them completely and totally for everything in every way. Watch as they fade away, their eyes are the last to disappear.

Take a moment here; recognize this is not about them changing, or doing something different or coming back into your life, or even changing if they are still in your life. And it doesn't mean you should go call them up right now either. In fact it might be a good idea to give this relationship some space, if you have not already. Take a couple of weeks or even a month if you can. This is for you, to release the past hurts and let it go. This is about you taking your power back and making that decision to forgive and forget all that has happened before now. Have you let it go?

If not, I want you to completely forgive them now, even if it seems painful and sad and *aren't they getting away with this?* No they are not getting away with anything, this is you getting free from the burden of this and no longer needing to carry it around with you. It's as if you hand the "back pack" you have been carrying around for years, back to them.

Can you let it go now fully and completely? Is your answer a resounding yes! As they fade completely away now, I would like you to take a moment and breathe into your tummy and expand it and allow all the feelings to move out of you. Feelings you have been holding there for a long time let them go now. If it's helpful, imagine those feelings running down your body, through the bottoms of your feet and directly down to the center of the earth where they are fully and completely consumed by the earth's molten center.

Imagine a great white cloud is coming down in front of you now, and I want you to search through and get all those old thoughts, images, sound tracks anything that had to do with those old feelings and experiences. Stuff them into that big cloud. Watch as it gets bigger and fatter. Now find the anger, and especially any rage. Look for those feelings of envy, jealousy, regret, pain and sadness. Now check around in case there is anything else left inside there. Get it all, and put it all into that big cloud and now watch as it drifts up to the sky, and towards the sun. It's going to touch the sun and implode completely releasing everything so there is *nothing left*.

There it goes now, gone completely. And breathing deeply, relax for a moment before you continue. Just absorb what has just happened. Congratulations… Well done!

This is the moment for you to reach deep inside of yourself and find the courage to forgive you. Take a moment find that sense of forgiveness again. Are you ready to give that same grace to you that you gave to the other? Perhaps for staying in that relationship or allowing those behaviors, or not taking care of yourself, or maybe even the times you used bulimia and knew you should not do this to yourself anymore. Forgive the lying, the cheating and even stealing behaviors that reinforced the bulimia.

Forgive yourself for all that has passed everything that happened or didn't happen, and all that troubled your heart so deeply. Especially forgive yourself if you continued to harm others with this behavior.

Forgive the shame and the guilt. Forgive the choices you made. Especially forgive yourself for believing that first lie about bulimia, that you could somehow, as if by magic, have all the cake you wanted and just get rid of it too. If it's too good to be true, generally it is.

Bulimia would not have so many negative side effects damaging your body and your mind and your soul the way it has done. There is nothing easy about bulimia, there never was. Bulimia was never a good idea in the first place, and the excessive restricting - forgive that too. I know it might have seemed like a good idea then, but you know the difference now: bulimia makes no sense at all.

It's yours to forgive yourself; no one else can do it for you. I want you to say the words out loud to yourself; *I forgive myself fully and completely, I am ready to let this go.*

Take a moment, sit with it, see what you see, hear what you hear, feel what you are feeling. Let it all go, can you? Do it? Just do it. Forgive it all. *Just say yes, I forgive it all, right now.* It doesn't mean it was right, that's not what forgiveness is. Forgiving lets us put this firmly in the past, heal and truly leave it in the past. Remember - the one good thing about the past: it is finally over.

Take a clearing breath, I know this is challenging, but you are the only one that can do this, and once you do, you will have acquired the "forgiveness tool" you can use for the rest of your life.

Good work. Now check for any other feelings or words that might be coming up. Release them into that second big cloud all the anger the hatred the frustration and the envy too, the jealousy, and even the judgment of yourself and others.

I'd like you to know that these internal thoughts or voices that are criticizing you, beating you up, holding you hostage daily to your past, are not from your higher self. Listen past that rabble to the deepest part of you and hear the clarity and compassion for you from your higher self.

Here you are home. Here you have faced yourself and your demons, and sometimes under very difficult circumstances. This is truly the definition of a hero.

Let it all go now. Can you, have you, let it all go?

I forgive myself for all of this, especially for the lies I told myself, and the times I went back against myself. I forgive myself fully and completely.

Is there anything else you need to forgive?

Take your time, just re-do the process, as often as you want, as often as needed.

If you are done, it's time to take those bits of paper rip them all up and safely burn them in the kitchen sink, or a fire place, just watch it all go to gray dust and ashes, and then turn the tap on and flush this down the drain *for the last time.*

Forgive yourself every day for everything, it is so freeing, and it feels so light. You are now truly finally really empty.

A time for connection to the deeper self- The empathic nature

Throughout my work, the empathic nature of clients with this disorder has shown up time and again. The empathic nature manifests in the ability to feel what others are feeling. Those sensory perceptions sometimes feel like those feelings are your own. If emotions are running high it's really hard to separate from the feelings and identify, is this mine? Or is it theirs? Sometimes it can feel like you know what others are feeling and sometimes it might seem: "these are my own feelings". This is the "empathic nature" and represents about 2% of the total population.

It will take a little more awareness, and that will come as you are kinder to yourself day to day and really appreciate the wonderful qualities you bring to this world. As you practice the perceptual positions more and more the easier it will become too.

You might remember back to the first time you sensed other people's feelings and thought they were yours. Those feelings felt very real and very intense. It might have been at school, perhaps at home or out at a family gathering.

One client thought she had been bulimic since the age of four. Her older sister broke a lamp and her father came to investigate. The sister blamed her and dad paddled her backside. She immediately ran into the bathroom and threw up; always believing this was the start of bulimia for her. What she had clearly done was release the negative energy she was feeling; the fear of the broken lamp, the anger over her sister's betrayal, and her father striking her. She never realized she was internalizing other people's feelings and then releasing the negative energy through vomiting. It was just her empathic nature.

These feelings you feel are often not yours, and it's confusing when trying to make sense of feelings that just seem to "come over you". Ever feel that sense of intense anger for no reason? Then you start looking for reasons to support the feelings. Wait; if they weren't yours in the first place...do you need to keep them? I believe if it was not your state in the first place, then simply discharge them - not mine!

How do we stop this kind of hyper-association about what others are doing, thinking or feeling? We really need to learn about boundaries. Sometimes in our families, our personal boundaries as children were not very well respected so we ended up unclear about what space was ours and what was someone else's. It can get confusing. In order to be "safe" in the world we over identify with others feelings and either emulate them, or make the feelings our own. We can even try to "help others" through becoming hyper-sensitive to what they are feeling, as a way of protecting ourselves.

Feelings are just feelings and everyone has them. Learning to identify what is yours and what belongs to someone else is the key to this one. It's a unique and beautiful aspect of who you are and valuable trait to have in our society today, where so many seem to act without ever thinking of others feelings.

However, as you well know when you are absorbing everyone else's feelings it can become overwhelming and exhausting. Instead simply ask yourself "Is this my feeling? No. It's not mine" and let it go.

One client learned this one just in time to help smooth out her new relationship. She had been sensing feelings for so long; it was startling to think that what she was feeling was not really about her.

She gathered her courage and began asking him what was up and realized pretty quickly what she used to believe was her, was his and only his. Often the mood swings were related to work issues, tiredness, or even a lack of food, her partner's mood swings no longer troubled her. She asked and clarified instead, saying to herself "nope, not me, not mine".

What would you like to do with your life?

What are your special gifts?

What did you want to be when you were about seven years old?

Today I choose to be at peace with myself.
Sounds a little like forgiveness to me.

CHALLENGE 9:

LIVING FROM GRATITUDE –
LIVING FROM THE HEART

The practice of gratitude and thankfulness are states of 'mindful' presence. You know you are here when you treat your body and the fuel you put into it with respect, gratitude and thankfulness. Inner awareness of your presence and the purpose of the food are to nourish your body. Be thankful for your mind; presence, awareness, gratitude in all things, especially thankful for the body and the food that nourishes you.

"Finally, I just wanted to express my sincere gratitude one more time. Kathy, thanks so much for all of your help and for everything you have done for me I'm grateful you never gave up on me"

This challenge is to hold a state of gratitude within every day, for your body, your mind and the food you feed it while tuning into the millions of little blessings that come your way every day.

Brene Brown suggests if we choose to live in the fearful state of what terrible thing will happen next, as a way to protect, or hedge against future disasters - we will miss the joy of life. We're terrified of joy; the moment joy is possible, something bad will certainly happen. Without gratitude we cannot fully engage the joy of our lives. A practice of gratitude grants us access to the joy in our lives.

Have you ever had one of those exciting moments, where you have succeeded and felt amazing about the moment? What is your first next thought? "Don't get too big for your britches"; "remember you still haven't….." And the laundry list pours forth on the moments of joy until everything is gone.

With awareness in the moment, we can stop and just for a moment feel the connection with an open heart for ourselves and experience the joy in that moment. How can we open our hearts in this way? *It's a choice point*, let's read on…

Michael Meade writes: the place where our wounds lay is right next to our genius. We're afraid of our wounds; we run from them, medicate and subdue them in addictions, all to avoid our genius.

If we stop the frantic behavior and play court to the quiet self, and listen to the ache in the heart as it cries out for peace, quiet and gentleness, we can begin to turn this around. Instead of focusing on the next bad thing, bring your awareness to this moment and allow gratitude to flood your mind and heart.

Who is guarding the sacred of your genius if it is not you? How do we regain access to the sacred space of the heart? It is said the heart holds our sacred truth, while the brain process's the rest of the systems.

The heart carries a sacred knowledge and wisdom and holds the connection to all we are.

Ask yourself these questions, and write out the responses you "hear". Ask the question until there are no more responses. This is a wonderful gift to you.

*   Who am I?
*   What are my gifts?

How do you know you are listening to the heart?

*   The heart speaks slowly
*   It only speaks in "present time"
*   It holds a deep wisdom about the situation
*   Sometimes we don't want to listen to the heart
*   The heart speaks in direct patterns
*   The heart does not blame others nor self
*   The heart observes with awareness and speaks with clarity

> *There is a knowing to the heart and a*
> *deep wisdom you can trust*

Mindful moments, following the breath

Spend some time practicing a more advanced form of conscious breathing. Get comfortable and close your eyes. Begin to imagine the breath as it flows in and out of the nostrils. After a few rounds of inhalations and exhalations, count to five on the inhale, hold the breath for five, and then exhale for a count of five. Do this several times for just a few minutes. After you've completed the exercise, rest for a minute or two. And notice now; as you breathe you want to be drawing the breath down into your belly. Imagine using your breath to inflate your tummy into a big balloon. At first it seems strange, and then it starts to feel good, keep breathing deeply into your body and see if you can take the breath right down to your hips and pelvis and then all the way down to your toes.

Breathing for balance

Today, we take a closer look at something we all do every day; breathe. Everything that is alive is energized by a force called Prana. Prana means energy or life force and for all sentient beings that life force is accessed through the breath. Deep breathing instantly puts you in touch with the flow of endorphins from the brain which down regulate the stress hormone cortisol. In other words you reverse the anxiety and panic, the fight or flight, the fear of what if, *just by breathing.*

Most of our breathing is regulated automatically; conscious breathing can completely shift our perception and release fear and anxiety. When we close our eyes and simply witness the breath as it flows in and out of our nostrils, we invite peace and balance into our lives, bathing our brain and every cell of our bodies with energy and vitality. Go ahead and try it right now. Just take a deep breath into your belly and kind of breathe your belly into a balloon, you are stretching the abdomen and helping it with oxygenated blood flow. This is "mindful breathing"… the mind is full of breath.

Our centering thought is: I am one with the breath of life

Gratitude holds power, and it's very personal, for only you can hold it. Holding gratitude for ourselves is literally granting us a daily blessing. And you can do this one for yourself. It's not dependent on any one else doing something or giving something to you. It's just for you, from you.

My gifts and finding them again

Enter the story board. This is an old practice but still one of the greatest ways to begin to find gratitude for your personal gifts; capturing pictures and words or sayings you appreciate about yourself and put them on a story board. Just pin them all up there.

What are your gifts? Today begin to build a story board for yourself. Find the things you deeply respect and value about yourself. Perhaps one of your gifts is you say it like it is. You speak your truth maybe your gift is never giving up maybe you have a time honored connection to helping others in need, maybe your gifts are working with children or teaching or maybe working with animals. No matter how we may have betrayed ourselves, our gifts are still there, they are the fabric of your soul, they will not be suppressed, and you know what they really are. Sometimes a family member may know and recognize our gifts, and we know who that family member is too. Go ask them for a list of your many gifts, and write them down.

Our Grace Bank Account:

Sometimes we let these simple things float by us and we think, *it's not much in the scheme of things*, but then *it is*. You noticed, you helped, smiled, and shared and if you hadn't, that moment would have been empty of your soul's signature. Yes, your soul has a signature, and you are writing with it every moment. What are you saying about your life today?

We cannot know how much our kindness to others impacts their lives. This is something we give freely and the grace created will always flow back to you. I like to call it our "grace bank account" and we can easily keep daily deposits up through simple acts of kindness and gratitude. And when things are really challenging those "deposits" are there to support us, even if we don't think to ask, someone or something wonderful happens and we are lifted to a new place in the moment. That's grace at work and it's always there to support us. Think back on your life to the times you were supported and you could not believe that wonderful act of kindness from some stranger as they touched your life just at the right moment when you needed it most.

Grace and Gratitude, they flow together.

Yes you can always ask your "grace bank account" for help. Just ask, it's there waiting to help you.

Appreciating my gifts, with gratitude

Starting my gratitude journal:

The next step in appreciating the gifts you have is the practice of gratitude: Being grateful for yourself, your body, your mind, your abilities, your work and your life. Take a few moments now and make a list of things you are grateful for. A way to start is asking: what am I grateful for right in this moment? Once you get into the habit of gratitude, you will start to see the incredible impact that awareness plays in your life. All of a sudden you begin to realize what you are grateful for is happening in your life more and more. You may even find the moments of awareness of gratitude really stop you now so you feel it in your heart and you just have to stop and think of the gratitude you are feeling.

How can you practice gratitude more often?
What is the tone of voice you would use for someone you were grateful for?
Can you use that same tone for yourself?
What about for something wonderful you have done?
What about members of your family?
How do you feel about your job?
How does holding that inner state of gratitude change how you feel about yourself?

Think of a time when you held that feeling of pure gratitude for someone, you were so grateful they were present in your life. What did that feel like? Did it make you smile, get teary or maybe feel like jumping for joy that you had someone like that in your life?

Remember the time, the place and get those good feelings rolling around inside your body. Now think about more things you feel grateful for, and add them to this feeling, amplify that feeling up to an 8 or 9 out of 10. How long you can hold it? Notice how it fills your lungs and you want to breathe right into that feeling, it's expansive and uplifting.

Gratitude

I'm doing it with you now, feeling this myself it seems to be centering on my heart and expanding with every breath. Can you feel it too? Anchor that feeling in yourself right now: "Gratitude for you"; and squeeze your thumb and finger together and add it to your other positive resource states.

I like to start my day: Mindful of gratitude and thankfulness

"The need to do more, to accomplish more is still in the back of my head. I've also still had some thoughts of binging on junk – chocolate covered almonds and a big bag of crunchy cheeses and diet pop. As you know this had been my past go to, easy binge food that I was using at work when I was still using bulimia. I had a brief moment yesterday in the afternoon where I thought

*of these foods. But the thoughts didn't last and don't have the
pull to go do it anymore."*

If we're honest we've been very focused on self-pleasuring
with our addictive behaviors. Gratitude is a gateway out of
these old patterns of behavior. Gratitude in the moment for
all that you have shifts the thinking from doing, to *being*

As we move beyond the old patterns of behavior, we are
not endeavoring to become more perfect, indeed no. We
are experiencing and focusing instead on the moments of
our lives that give us dynamic connection to all there is…
through gratitude.

We're beyond those old behaviors now, and those flash back
moments ask us to bring ourselves into right alignment
with what our purpose is. It's the call to go beyond our
own comfort zone into our own greatness and begin to
play out our rightful role within the divine plan of our
universe. It's time to awaken to the needs of others and
the love that we can provide to help others heal and secure
wholeness themselves and in doing so; we achieve the same
for ourselves. What we give, we receive.

When these flashbacks of old behavior happen, and
sometimes it can happen in dream time. It's not because
you are weakening, or that you will give into this behavior
again. It's because your deep self is clearing at the deepest
levels of your psyche. Grateful now as you are nearly done
with this completely.

Flashbacks can be scary and the easiest way to deal with them is to quickly recognize it's just an old image, and old feeling. Take the color out of those images, cancel the thought with "so what, it's just an old thought".

And it may be time for us to lead the way. Lead ourselves out of this into the life we want. As we begin to evolve and practice using these tools to help ourselves. It will become clearer as to how we can reach out to others and begin to serve in ways we never dreamed possible. It's not about repaying the waste but through forgiveness and the practice of gratitude now it's time to begin to find ways to be of service to others and the life we are here to live.

Gratitude is the awareness of the deep flow of life's eternal calling, and you are a part of it all.

EXERCISE FOR THIS CHALLENGE Love as a choice point – this little exercise was created through Mastery of Deep Trance States® and helps us engage the heart and listen to our own deep wisdom:

There are two major centers of intelligence within all of us; the brain and the heart. Often the heart is disregarded as distant second cousin; the cause of pain and suffering and the feelings that make one want to run away from love or heart centered connections. But wait, consider this: Is it not the head that reasons, argues and creates disjointed belief strategies? Is it not the head that wants control, argues imperfections, and sabotages relationships? Is it not the deep wisdom of the heart that helps us eventually heal from all we've been telling ourselves?

The brain is a fantastic record keeper and can produce evidence in the moment to support a decision or feeling. It recalls everything from the past, and projects those experiences into a fearful anxious future. It's fast, efficient and will delete and distort any experience to support a current theory as to how or why something is the way it is. Stories: just endless stories of what if, when, who, how, where…it's endless. The mind is endless and tenacious in its efforts to sway us. New evidence appears and the mind quickly jumps ship to the other side of the argument: "of course this is the way to go, we knew it all along." The mind can also be mindless, and behave mindlessly encouraging behaviors that are incongruent with who we really are, and vastly out of alignment with our heart-centered desires.

The heart speaks in a very different way. It doesn't consider the past or the future, but remains in the present moment. Its comments are slow, shorter and void of negativity. The heart is the access to your deep wise self. It speaks slower, and is often lost completely in the frenzy of the busy mind. The heart offers us a "choice point". A consideration based in deeper wisdom.

We can stop in the moment; take that brain comment which is running away with our feelings, emotions and beliefs; stop, and listen to what the heart says. I know it sounds ridiculously simple, if this works why doesn't everyone do it? Those addictions to the pain body, the drama of life, the intensity of creating drama giving importance to oneself or ones beliefs, the ego, the "little me" as Eckhart Tolle names it. This is often how wars start, the argument of brain overwhelms the reality of the moment, and everything is lost. Think back along your own past, are there any inner arguments you convinced yourself were absolutely true?

Here's one *"I'm so upset with my body, my shape and how I look. Everyone else is having so much fun, because they look thinner than I do. I have fat legs and hips, if I was thinner, everyone would like me more."* As these arguments and negative assaults continue, you become more and more downcast, insular, and reject anyone's attempts to dissuade you. You sense everyone sees you differently, you don't fit in, you feel overwhelmed and your brain is now going a million miles a second…

As you increase your anxiety and tension, fears and worries, your heart would be receiving adrenaline to pump faster and harder, to help you run away from this obviously stressful moment. It would shorten breath and increase heart rates to activate you even more. Time to run away!

Stop right there, and lets just slow this down. Deep breaths will relax the heart rate, and send more oxygen to the blood stream, relaxing tight muscles and easing the panic feelings. What however, are your thoughts doing? Brain is still convinced something bad is going on, until you interrupt that negativity and redirect it.

Speaking from the heart:

- Think a thought… now imagine placing that thought into your heart space and listen…
- Notice the heart speaks in present time, it does not project into the future, nor does it reflect on the past, and it speaks slowly

The best practice is to practice, the steps are easy: think the thought, imaging placing that thought in your heart and listen. What does it say to you? If it's not in present time, it's still coming from your thinking mind. Try this out in your day when things are challenging or you feel a little overwhelmed. Stop, place your thoughts into your heart and listen.

A typical Mind Thought: I'm feeling really anxious about ….?

A typical Heart response: *Listen what does your heart say?*

I start my day with gratitude and thankfulness. As I open my eyes each day I find my mind focusing on things I'm grateful for. It might be the simplest thing, like gratitude for the bed that supports me. Use this heart centered awareness to bring deeper compassion, self-care and self-love into your life every day. The most important person you need validation from is yourself.

In the second 30 day period add to this gratitude list:

I'm grateful for my body, my brain, and my heart. I know how to listen to my heart and I know it's just a choice point I can choose differently any time I want to.

In the third 30 day period add to your gratitude list:

I'm grateful for my family: my mother and father who gave me life, without them I would not be here. I'm grateful for their support in my life. (Even if they are no longer with you physically, their energy continues to support you).

I'm grateful for the air I breathe, and the water I consume the Earth that supports me.

I'm grateful for the minerals and nutrients the Earth provides me with every day.

I'm grateful for my work and my mind and that I can participate in this life.

I know as I am healing from all this, I'm grateful I can shift my focus to what is going very right for me; moment to moment things are improving.

I'm grateful I can focus on the gratitude I feel for my recovery.

I'm grateful for those that have come into my life to help me.

I am grateful I can solve and resolve problems and I'm grateful for my mind.

I know I feel better every day and in every way; my life is getting better and better. I don't have to be perfect, and I don't have to do this perfectly either.

As I feel these feelings and hold these kinds of thoughts it is easy for me to appreciate myself even more than I did even just a few moments ago. As I take a deep in drawn breath I'm ready to rise and greet this wonderful day, wondering what amazing things are coming my way today. I daily embrace gratitude.

Gratitude and thankfulness is from the heart. Bring your awareness to the center of your chest, and breathe into it. As you expand the chest feel yourself connecting to your own heart, the center of your compassion. Without compassion for yourself you cannot offer this to others. Without self-love we cannot love another. "As I love myself, I love another."

Start your day for the next 90 days with three things you are grateful for and keep a little journal of your daily gratitude. It's amazing how this will change your life.

EXERCISE FOR THIS CHALLENGE

Awareness is everything. This simple quiz can help you become more heart centered in your life.

- Have you already looked ahead on this test?
- Do you need to keep busy all the time?
- Would others say you walk, drive or move fast?
- Do you have little rituals designed to 'save time'?
- Do you *ah ha* when others talk trying to hurry them up?
- Are you a lane jumper in traffic?
- Are you usually finished eating before everyone else?
- Are you often swearing or angry while driving?
- Do you talk fast, gasping for air or spraying or getting tongue tied?
- Do you try to hurry others speaking by nodding or interrupting them?
- Do you tilt your head, raise eyebrows, and roll your eyes to get others to speed up?
- Do you push elevator buttons that are already lit?
- Are you cynical and distrusting of others?
- Do you have sleep stress, snoring, grinding of teeth, tossing and turning?
- Do you replay angry events to rehearse what you will say, or spread negative war stories?
- Do you have family, marital conflicts and/or neglect your family?
- Once you have achieved that success, or attained a goal, do you feel let down, lost and without direction?

- Was there never enough unconditional love from your parents?
- When you listen to the sound of your voice, is it critical or sarcastic in quality?
- Do you use your laughter and public displays of emotion as attention seeking?
- Do you react emotionally, defensively, and negatively to comments from others?
- Is meditation challenging for you because you are restless or even fall asleep when sitting quietly?
- Do you answer questions before they're completely asked?
- Do you always feel your way is the right way?

Heart Energy: Score each response: 0 = Never; 1 = Almost Never; 2= More than Sometimes; 3 = A Lot; 4= almost always Score Grid: 0-10 you are in your heart most of the time; 10-20 practice consciously connecting with your heart; 20-35 practice daily with gratitude and listening to your heart; 35 + embrace this challenge as your new life path and start today

Today I am grateful for all that I am.

Today I am thankful for my life, my body, my brain, my soul. Today I am grateful that my body knows how to heal itself and I'm thankful to let it do just that.

SHARING FROM OTHERS ALONG THE PATH TO WELLNESS:

I still get pent up by people getting too much in my personal space and annoyed I know this is just part of feeling emotions and will continue to practice letting the feelings/energies ebb and flow, welcoming the knowledge to be gained from riding the wind.

Honestly I was afraid of the outcome and having to do it over again because "once again no one can assist me in finding the source of the discord, I'm a lost cause".

We did some life shattering/soul affirming work together. The conversations with you, the love-infused nourishment, the embracing room, the first place I came home... In essence you're a midwife of souls.

Thank you for caring, listening, your enthusiasm; I am very different.

My father e-mailed me last night, an extensively sharing spontaneous letter. It feels so good to TRULY forgive him and my brother. What freedom...

My eternal gratitude for you in guiding me with such wisdom in finding my true hunger, my authentic self, we did soul retrieval. May I always know you... may our journeys both open up to rainbows of prismatic colour."

"I'm on my way and the toughest part was those earlier days, as my thoughts were a little stiff, but nothing I couldn't handle. And I just plugged away and enjoyed myself. Never looking too far ahead, never thinking too much about what was ahead.

Sometimes with the little sayings in my head, just keep going, I can do it, I can do it just little things to keep going that have worked previously for me. Things I know to do when I'm facing challenges that ask me to rise above the moment. There were no real parts that were overly difficult when approached as little bits of the overall goal, completing one day at a time.

I was unsure what the following months were going to be like, because I hadn't done this for that amount of time before. I had thoughts, but nothing I couldn't handle and there were no real parts where I felt like I didn't want to go on or anything. There were more challenges and thoughts, and yet I actually felt better than the first month, many times.

I visited with others as I challenged some of the bigger issues, which got me through those ones without really thinking or worrying about going on or whatever else might have come into my head. The whole time stopping at different times, having a little food, refilling as needed. Food is my fuel, whatever I needed to do and then just went onto the next and in the end I know lots of people are cheering me on. I feel pretty good and

I'm not sure when I actually finished but I stopped, celebrated, I'm having a great life. Sometimes I'm tired, but I know I don't have to do it all in one day. Just happy at how my body performed, consistently and completed what I've been wanting all along. That's it to report for now."

30 days in a row into my successful recovery never thought it could happen but it has!

Making the decision and committing to be healthy, without sugar and exercising daily has been the answer! Life is work! It is not easy (since we are constantly evolving), but I know the new healthy patterns will become more routine and it will get easier. I took the easy way out for 30 years but the pay off now is being in control of my life finally! Thank you Kathy

"I'm feeling fabulous and started a yoga challenge. I find myself enjoying a good work out from time to time mixed in with more gentle yoga. It's great because I'm finding that I am gentle with myself and my body. Love it"

Just a quick note...

I have been constant in my daily listening to the Cd's, meditation, tapping, my time for visualizing and also for gratitude and my daily affirmations. I pretty much eat the 5-6 small meals a day.

I shut my TV off when i am not actually watching it. I sleep without the TV now

I am writing down my feelings & they are mostly gratitude.

I have rewarded myself with manicures, pedicures, shopping, etc. instead of food.

My husband is quite proud! I took another day off of running. My weight was up a bit, but I know our bodies fluctuate from day to day so I decided it's best to not weigh, but listen to my body.

The first 10 days were the hardest, but it is so nice to finally picture a more peaceful life!

Thanks again.

This is an awesome idea and so simple, yet I feel it… like tingles all over.

It took me less than a minute at my desk to close my eyes, ask for the soul that I am – the one without bulimia – and there's something that floods over me… I just feel different. As for how I am doing? GREAT!!! I'm eating and not "vomiting" Oh Kathy I think you saved my life :)"

I just wanted to send you a hug and thanks,

I am truly grateful for everything you have done for my daughter - it has given her - her life back, and she's been doing so much better now :-) She will be coming home to ski for a week in January, and I'm really looking forward to seeing her then… (I know her heath is improving, because she finally got her monthly cycle back (whenever she needs a "tune-up" I hope she'll come back to see you)

Just wanted to say I have been in the best mood these past few days and I'm not really sure why. I have been eating healthy and not tempted to engage. I have been social and productive and happy. I just feel like a different person. I am really trying to remind myself that my Ed wastes so much time. Precious time I don't have to spare. I'm not fully happy with my weight but I am reminding myself that it's not the defining aspect of me as a person. It's nice to be in this mindset. I'm not saying I'm fully recovered or anything but I just feel different. I've also not been going to group lately either because I'd rather do something fun instead of reminding myself I have a problem... It's probably just distracting me but right now I'm okay with that.

THE 90 DAY CHALLENGE QUICK NOTES:

Three small meals a day, three small snacks in between

Use portion sizes that are right there in your hands
Thickness and size of the palm of your hand for protein size
One cupped hand for size for cooked carbohydrates
Two cupped hands together for veggies or raw salad portion
sizes
Protein rich eating proteins first
Eat between 7 am and 7 pm daily to optimize your
metabolism

Avoid junk sugar – read your labels and clear your kitchen
of junk sugars

Eat vegetables and fruit as they contain the whole glucose
molecule needed for your brain

Exercise 3-4 times a week, 20 minutes is all you need, more
is not better; it's often just more

Lots of water daily (6-8 glasses)

Avoid the use of alcohol and drugs, they cloud your
thinking and carry the wrong energy vibration for your

sensitive nature. They will also increase cravings and sugar sensitivity

80/20 rule – 80 % of the meal, the day, the week the month, follow this balanced eating plan; 20% of the meal the day, the week the month, you have room for deviations. This creates balance and flexibility reducing 'all or nothing thinking' and getting you out of "rule bounded thinking" of measuring, weighing, and restricting behaviors that challenge recovery

Listen to the MP3s and Cd's

Join a weekly yoga class or meditation group

Shop from a list, eat before you shop, eat before you eat with others

Personal meditation practice

Set up a space in your house for daily meditation

This signals the brain for meditation & relaxation which offsets stress hormones

Adopt an inner re-frame that **Food is Fuel, Food is just fuel,** *I eat to live, and I don't live to eat.*

Take your supplements

Be kind to yourself – re-frame anything negative that is harmful to your progress

Smile in the mirror at least 3 times a day

Practice: Use your "thumb & finger anchors" for good feelings every day

Gratitude and thankful every day and in every way

And just when the caterpillar thought her world was over,
She turned into a beautiful butterfly

RECOMMENDED READING:

MINDSET: by Carole Dweck

MOTHER DAUGHTER WISDOM: by Dr. Christiane Northrup

THE WORLD BEHIND THE WORLD: by Michael Meade

THE FOUR AGREEMENTS: by D. M. Ruiz

AMEN SOLUTION: by Dr. AMEN,

THE EDGE EFFECT: by Eric Breberman

THE PALEO SOLUTION – by Robb Wolf

THE EAT CLEAN DIET- by Tosca Reno

Link to the poem "The Journey" by Mary Oliver
http://peacefulrivers.homestead.com/maryoliver.html

Films and documentaries:

Miss Representation - You-tube

Mother Daughter Wisdom - Dr. C. Northrup

FED UP- a movie about the Sugar Industry

"SUGAR" - documentary by Fifth Estate and available on line

RESOURCES:

http://www.waysofthewisewoman.com
www.chasinghunger.com

The Bulimia Breakthrough Method™ "Kathy Welter Nichols is a pioneer in this work; she's an absolute expert in her area, tackling this very challenging area using Hypnosis and NLP" One of the very few people working with bulimia in her ground breaking Bulimia Breakthrough Method®

Overcome Bulimia, two MP3 Set

MP3's support your recovery – find them on my web site at www.waysofthewisewoman.com

CHASING HUNGER – Affirmations Card Set

Packed with daily tips and reminders, Just pick a card every day and follow the suggestion, knowing your deep self knows just what you need Available now on http://www.chasinghunger.com/?page_id=91

CPSIA information can be obtained at www.ICGtesting.com
Printed in the USA
LVOW07s0254230715

447220LV00001B/1/P